THE PARTHENON

EVERYDAY LIFE IN ANCIENT GREECE

BY

C. E. ROBINSON

Assistant Master at Winchester College

GREENWOOD PRESS, PUBLISHERS
WESTPORT, CONNECTICUT

Library of Congress Cataloging in Publication Data

Robinson, Cyril Edward, 1884-
    Everyday life in ancient Greece.

    Reprint of the 1933 ed. published by the
Clarendon Press, Oxford.
    Includes index.
    1. Greece--Social life and customs.   I.   Title.
[DF78.R63   1978]   938   77-27627
ISBN 0-8371-9078-9

Reprinted in 1978 by Greenwood Press,
A division of Congressional Information Service, Inc.
88 Post Road West, Westport, Connecticut 06881

Library of Congress catalog card number 77-27627
ISBN 0-8371-9078-9

Printed in the United States of America

10 9 8 7 6 5 4

PREFACE

THERE is a story told of a certain English poet, who, as an undergraduate at Oxford, was compelled to undergo an examination in Divinity. His upbringing had not included a study of the Bible; and his preparation for the examination had been wofully inadequate. When, therefore, he was asked to translate from the Greek Testament the passage describing the shipwreck of St. Paul, he read it for the first time. After he had translated a few verses with tolerable success, one of the examiners announced that that would do. 'No, sir, it will not do,' was the surprising answer, 'I want to know what happened to the beggar.' Its irreverence and impudence apart, nothing could have been more admirable than that rejoinder. It was wholly in keeping with the spirit of the Greeks; and it is to be hoped that this book will be read, and the study of Greek civilization further pursued by those who read it, with the same vigorous zest for inquiry.

C. E. R.

Sept. 1933.

LIST OF DATES

c. 2300–1600 B.C.   Civilization developed in Peloponnese, &c., under Cretan influence.

c. 1600–1250 B.C.   Golden Age of Mycenaean civilization.

c. 1250   Greek-speaking Achaeans begin to arrive from north.

c. 1180.   Trojan War. [Israelites enter Canaan.]

c. 1100–1000.   Invasion of Dorian Greeks from north, and migrations to coast of Asia Minor.

c. 900.   Homeric Poems written down. [Solomon King in Israel.]

c. 800 onwards.   Formation of Greek City-states; and plantation of numerous 'colonies' on Aegean coasts, south Italy, Sicily, &c.

c. 750.   [Foundation of Rome.]

c. 720.   Sparta's conquest of Messenia.

c. 650–630.   Revolt of Messenia followed by Lycurgan Reform.

550–500.   Sparta wins supremacy of Peloponnese.

586.   [Fall of Jerusalem. Jews go into exile in Babylonia.]

570–510.   Athens under 'tyranny' of Pisistratus and his sons.

508.   Athens becomes a democracy. [Rome becomes a republic.]

490.   First Persian Invasion defeated at Marathon.

480–479.   Second Persian Invasion by Xerxes, battles of Thermopylae, Salamis, and Plataea.

479–454.   Delian Confederacy develops into Athenian Empire.

438.   Completion of Parthenon.

431–421.   First Phase of Peloponnesian War (Pylos, &c.).

415–413.   Athenian Expedition against Syracuse.

413–404.   Second phase of Peloponnesian War (Aegospotami 405) and Fall of Athens.

390.   [The Gauls sack Rome.]

338.   Athens and Thebes defeated at Chaeronea by Philip of Macedon.

334–325.   Alexander of Macedon conquers the East.

323.   Death of Alexander.

CONTENTS

LIST OF ILLUSTRATIONS

THE CHAMBER OF ATREUS AT MYCENAE
A building erected by the Greeks of the Homeric age.

I

LIFE IN THE HEROIC AGE

ONE reason why we are still interested in the ancient Greeks is that they have left behind them a literature of unrivalled beauty and wisdom. To produce a great literature a great language is needed; and the Greeks were fortunate in possessing a language at once so flexible and so musical that it could express every shade of meaning and emotion as perhaps no other language has ever done. In this language of theirs the Greeks, then, composed masterpieces of poetry, drama, philosophy, rhetoric, and history which can still stir the wonder and the imagination of mankind. Only those who can read them in the original can appreciate their full beauty and depth; but even through English translations it is possible to learn something of what the Greeks thought and felt and what manner of lives they led.

Side by side with their writings, moreover, they left behind them other products of their artistic genius—stately temples, graceful sculptured statues, delicate painted pottery, and metal ornaments. These, too, we can use to supplement the knowledge which comes to us from written records.

Such knowledge as we possess of the earliest phase of Greek history is drawn from both sources. Some time in the thirteenth century before Christ a tribe of Greek-speaking[1] folk who called themselves Achaeans came down from eastern Europe into the peninsula which we now call Greece. This peninsula they found inhabited by an ancient people who had already reached a high state of civilization, closely connected with the still more ancient civilization of the adjacent island of Crete. They found lordly castles built on hill-tops and surrounded by massive walls of

---

[1] The Greeks called themselves 'Hellenes'. The name Greek was applied to them first by the inhabitants of Italy.

huge 'Cyclopean' boulders; and somehow or other—probably not by warlike capture—they succeeded in making these fortresses their own. Examples of such fortresses may still be seen at Tiryns and Mycenae in the Argive Plain; and from the

FIG. 1. MAP TO ILLUSTRATE GREECE IN HOMERIC TIMES

remains of their palaces which archaeologists have unearthed we are able to learn something of the splendid style in which the Achaean princes lived. But they were a restless folk; and not long content with a life of prosperous peace, they took ship

SUBTERRANEAN GALLERY, TIRYNS (*see opposite*)

This gallery is constructed in the thickness of the walls, which at their base (below the ground-level of the citadel) are a dozen yards in width. The masonry consists of huge 'Cyclopean' boulders skilfully piled to form a rude pointed vault. Side openings off the gallery lead into store-chambers.

FIG. 2. SUBTERRANEAN GALLERY, TIRYNS

and crossed the sea in search of plunder. The most famous of their expeditions was against the city of Troy, which lay on the north-west corner of Asia Minor hard by the Dardanelles. Concerning this and other exploits their minstrels composed songs, and the songs were treasured, being handed down, as we may guess, from minstrel father to minstrel son. By and by the Greeks learnt the art of writing from Phoenician merchants; and about 900 B.C. a certain poet called Homer—a blind old bard, so later tradition said—strung many of these songs together to form two great poems called the *Iliad* and the *Odyssey*, the most thrilling and beautiful tales that were ever told in verse.[1] It is from these two poems, as well as from the remains which archaeologists have dug up, that we know how the Greeks lived in this early age before the dawn of history proper.

The Achaean princes kept great style. Their palaces, indeed, as may be seen at Mycenae and Tiryns, were simply planned. A spacious hall or 'Megaron' was their living-room, with a central hearth surrounded by four pillars which propped the roof, the smoke escaping through a vent-hole overhead. Here, too, the men slept, while the womenfolk retired to quarters of their own. Outside the ante-chamber of the hall lay an open courtyard, surrounded by a penthouse or veranda where slaves

---

[1] The *Iliad* relates a series of episodes in the great Trojan War, culminating in the story of the mortal combat in which the Greek Achilles slew the Trojan champion Hector and dragged the corpse at his chariot-tail around the city walls. The *Odyssey* tells of the homeward voyage of the Greek Odysseus (called Ulysses by the Romans) to his native town on the island of Ithaca, where he found his faithful wife Penelope hard pressed and his substance wasted by a crowd of insolent suitors, among whom he entered in the guise of a poor beggar, but presently seizing a bow, disclosed himself and shot them down in his own halls.

A 'HOMERIC' CUP (*see opposite*)

One of two gold cups found at Vaphio. The scene is a bull-hunt; a girl has locked arms and legs round the bull's horns while, beneath, a cow-boy has apparently been tossed.

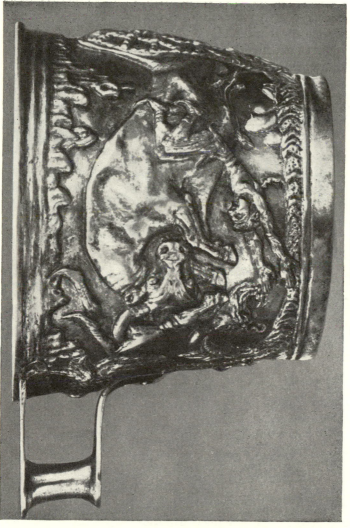

Fig. 3. A 'HOMERIC' CUP

and even guests might be set to sleep. Besides other rooms and store chambers there was usually a bath-room; for the Achaeans were a cleanly folk and always after travel or fighting would take their first opportunity of a good wash. But though simple in structure, their palaces were handsomely adorned. In one has been found the remains of a beautiful patterned frieze of alabaster inlaid with blue glass. One may guess that even in the fairy-tale description which Homer gives of the palace of King Alcinous some of the detail has been drawn from actual life. *'Brazen were the walls on this side and on that, and round about them ran a frieze of blue; and golden were the doors which enclosed that goodly house, with door posts of silver on a threshold of bronze and a silver lintel above, and on either side stood golden dogs and silver to guard the house of great-hearted Alcinous. Within were seats set in array along the wall, and thereupon were spread delicate coverlets fine woven, the women's handiwork. Moreover there were youths fashioned in gold, standing on firm-set bases with flaming torches in their hands, giving light through the night to feasters in the palace.'*

The craftsmen of those days, we know, were extremely skilful, and worked in rich materials. Gold is constantly mentioned. As in the days of King Solomon, silver was 'little accounted of'. Bronze was the favourite metal; and iron was as yet a rarity. A famous pair of drinking-cups has been discovered, both of beaten gold; and on one the scene of a bull-hunt, on the other a herd of oxen are depicted with a skill which beggars fancy. Homer, too, tells of a shield, manufactured for Achilles, on which were graven or inlaid all manner of scenes taken from daily life. It is from these scenes, as he describes them, that we can gain perhaps the best picture of how the Achaeans lived.

Agriculture was naturally one of the chief means of livelihood. The staple products of the soil were corn, wine, and oil which was pressed from olive-berries and served the ancients in place of butter for cooking and of soap for washing. Ploughing was done with teams of oxen or mules. Here is the picture which we get from Achilles' shield:

> *And thereafter on the shield*
> *He set a tender fallow-field;*
> *Passing rich the tillage was*
> *And three times worked and wide,*
> *And in it wheeling up and down*
> *A-many ploughmen plied*
> *Their teams; and when anon they drew*
> *Unto the fallow's end,*
> *Then came a man to meet them there*
> *And gave into their hand*
> *Wine in a goblet honey-sweet;*
> *So turned they up the furrow*
> *And were full fain to come again*
> *To the end of the deep fallow.*

Next the harvesting:

> *And next a lord's domain deep-soiled*
> *He set thereon and in it toiled*
> *Hireling reapers; in their hands*
> *Sharp sickles they were plying.*
> *And down the furrow fell the swathes,*
> *Some well in order lying*
> *And some the binders bound with straw;*
> *For binders there were three,*
> *And boys behind them plucked and bore*
> *By armfuls for to give them store*
> *And the work went on unceasingly.*
> *And thereamong the overlord*
> *In silence, hand on stave,*
> *Was standing by the furrow's edge*
> *And the heart in him was blithe.*

Far more than on agriculture, however, the Achaeans depended for their livelihood on the pasturage of flocks and herds. They kept goats, sheep, and swine; but their most prized possession was the ox, an animal doubly useful for ploughing as well as for food. In this primitive age when coined money was not yet invented, they even measured values by so many head of oxen; and many female names, such as Alphesiboea 'the winner of oxen', disclose the fact that at the time of the child's birth the anxious father had looked forward to his daughter's marriage-day when she would bring him some return for the cost of her upbringing. On Achilles' shield the oxen are not forgotten:

> *A herd of straight-horned kine anon*
> *He did fashion thereupon;*
> *Of gold and tin were the kine chased*
> *And with lowing loud they paced*
> *From the midden to the mead*
> *By rippling river and waving reed.*
> *And golden-wrought beside the kine*
> *Went drovers four, and with them nine*
> *Fleet-footed hounds were following;*
> *But among the cows ahead*
> *Two lions terrible and dread*
> *A mighty bull held bellowing.*
> *Loud roared he, as they dragged him down*
> *And the young swains and dogs made haste*
> *To aid him; but they two had torn*
> *The hide of the great bull to taste*
> *The entrails and black blood. In vain*
> *The drovers urged the swift dogs on;*
> *But they in fear shrank back again*
> *And cowering there gave tongue.*

Olive-picking was a humdrum task; but the vintage was a fit theme for poetry.

Fɪɢ. 4. OLIVE TREES

And a vineyard cluster-laden
Next he fashioned fair and golden;
Black hung the bunches, standing high
On silver poles continuously.
And around, a ditch of azure
And a pale he drave of tin;
And up it ran a single path,
By the which to gather in
The vintage would the pickers pass.
Merry hearted lad and lass
In baskets bore the honeyed fruit;
Among them on a shrilling lute
A boy made witching melody
And chanted sweet in piping voice
The Linus Song: so tripped they on
With music and with merry noise.

All this makes a happy and pleasant picture of peaceful country life. But the Achaeans were no stay-at-homes. The love of excitement was strong in them, and in part it was satisfied by the pleasures of the chase. The Homeric poems are full of allusions to hunting—hares and deer and wild boars; there were even frequent encounters with lions. But this was not enough for their restless spirit. Greece is a sea-girt country with many creeks and inlets offering good harbourage, and innumerable scattered islands through which ships might thread their way with security in summer. So the Achaeans, and the other Greeks after them, took readily to the sea. Launching their gaily painted galleys 'of the scarlet cheek' and 'sitting well in order on the thwarts' they would 'smite the grey sea with their oars' and so fare forth on their adventures. Many went in quest of trade, penetrating distant corners of the Mediterranean waters. Traffic with Egypt and the Levant was common; and Phoenician merchantmen brought to Greek shores many valuables and luxuries from the East.

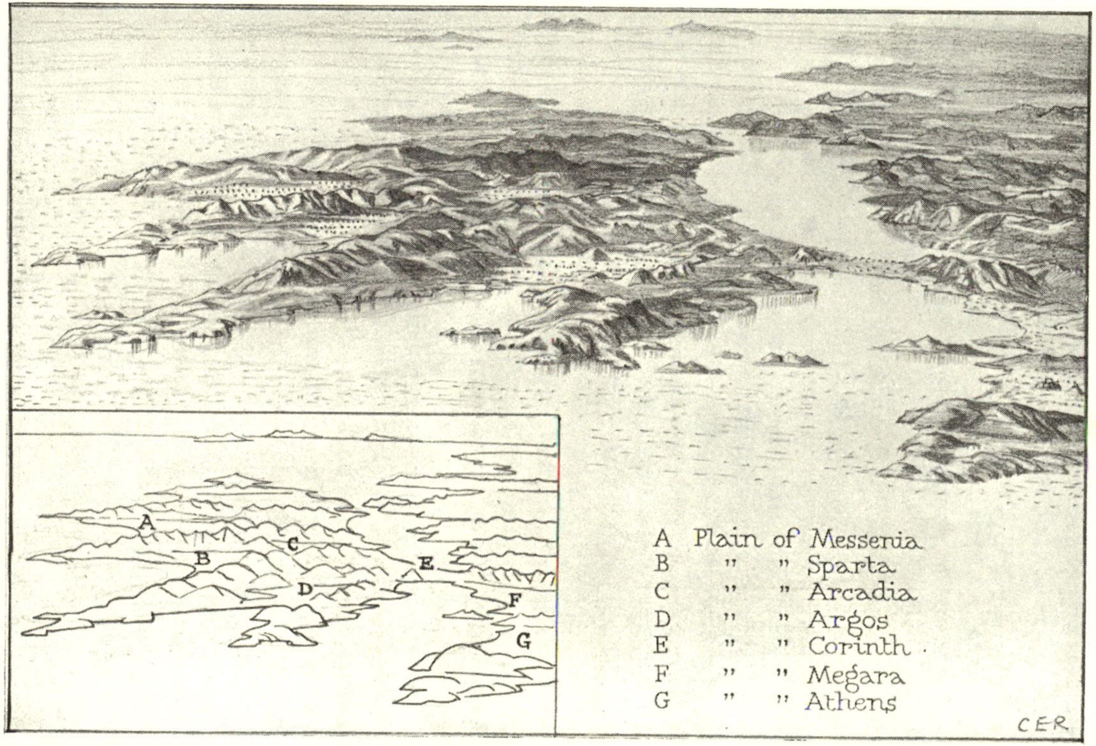

A Plain of Messenia
B " " Sparta
C " " Arcadia
D " " Argos
E " " Corinth
F " " Megara
G " " Athens

CER

Fig. 5. A rough bird's-eye view of Greece from the south-east. Note the level plains nestling between the mountain chains and the numerous inlets and islands.

But more often the Greeks themselves would sail in search of plunder. Here is a tale from Homer—the tale of an imaginary adventurer, but none the less true to fact. '*Labour of the field I never loved, nor home-keeping thrift, but galleys with their oars were dear to me and wars and trim spears and darts. Nine times had I been a leader of men and of swift-faring ships against a strange folk and wealth fell ever to my hand. Then the people called on me to lead the ships to Troy and there we sons of the Achaeans warred nine years and in the tenth year sacked the city and fared home. One month alone I abode with my children and my gentle wife and then my spirit bade me fit out our ships and sail to Egypt with my goodly company. On the fifth day we came to the fair flowing river Aegyptus and I bade my companions abide there with the ships and guard them and sent forth scouts to spy upon the land. But my men in their folly fell to wasting the fields of the Egyptians and haled off their wives and children and put their men to the sword. Whereat the battle cry was raised within the city and the folk came forth and slew many of us and others they led up with them alive to work for them in durance.*' It reads like the description of some Viking raid.

The Achaeans then were great warriors, and of their method of fighting something must needs be said. Some used the bow; some even hurled great boulders so heavy that 'not two men could lift them nowadays'. But the spear was the favourite weapon. Armour consisted of bronze helmet with 'waving horse-hair plume'; a leather or metal cuirass; bronze greaves for the legs; and a shield formed of a huge ox-hide stretched on wooden struts and strengthened with boss or layers of bronze. With this weighty accoutrement the warrior was ill able to travel afoot to the battle-field; so he drove in a chariot—horses were used in harness, but never ridden at this date—then leaving his squire to handle the steeds, dismounted and engaged some hostile champion in single combat. The two crouched behind their enveloping shields, from cover of which they launched their 'ashen spears' till one or other was wounded. The issue of the battle was usually decided by such single combats. The common folk were only lightly armed and could make no stand against the prowess of the champions, before

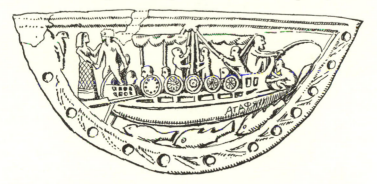

Fig. 6. An ancient ship taken from an early ivory-carving and similar to ships described in Homer. In the centre two men haul at the mainsail which is furled to a yard-arm. The rowers sit each behind his shield. In prow and stern are short decks; from one a man is fishing; from the other the captain says good-bye to his wife. The steersman, seated astern, wields two paddles.

whom they were as chaff before the wind. Here is Homer's picture of Achilles' passage through the mêlée:

> *As down the hollow of the glen*
> *Fierce fire its havoc plays,*
> *When drought is on the mountain*
> *And the deep woods are ablaze,*
> *And a wind blows which catcheth up*
> *And hunts the flame all ways;*
> *So all ways ravening with his spear,*
> *As he had been a god's own peer,*
> *He hunted and he slew them there,*
> *Till earth ran black where the blood was.*
> *And, as when broad-browed bulls are yoked*

White barley for to tread,
Upon a threshing-floor well-lain
And 'neath the feet of lowing kine
Is lightly sifted out the grain,
So by high-souled Achilles sped
The hoovèd horses trod the shield
And trampled on the dead.
Below upon the axle-tree
And above about the rail
The chariot dripped with a bloody froth,
It spurted from the horses' hoof,
It spurted from the wheel;
So did the son of Peleus ride
For winning of the battle's pride;
And in the carnage deep he dyed
His hands invincible.

As in war, so in peace, the common folk counted for little. This was what we call a 'patriarchal' age—that is, the political power in the community lay in the hands of the 'fathers' or heads of families. The chief or prince, as 'father' of the tribe, commanded its host in war, sacrificed to the gods for its common welfare, and sat in judgement upon disputes among its members. Often he called the other leading men or elders into consultation. Homer gives us a picture of these elders met together in the market-place to settle a blood-feud.

In the mart the folk were thronging
Where had arisen strife,
Two men striving for the ransom
Upon a dead man's life;
And one averred that all was quit
To the folk attesting it;
But one that he had gotten naught,
And both before a justice sought

Trial of their suit; and loud
The backers cried for either side
But heralds stayed the crowd.
On smooth stones in a holy ring
The elders sat, and in their hands
Heralds of the lusty voice
Had set the sacred wands,
Wherewith stood they forth in turn
Each to say his say
And sooth it is that in the midst
Two golden talents lay
To give to him among them all
Who should judge of it most right.

It is of the life of these chiefs and leaders that the Homeric poems for the most part tell. Occasionally we get a glimpse of the life of the lesser folk. The *Odyssey*, in particular, relates many incidents which throw a light on their condition. It tells of beggars who haunt the courts of the rich, of a Phoenician slave-woman who was beguiled by the trinkets of a Levantine pedlar into eloping on his ship, of men kidnapped from their homes and sold into bondage. Of one slave, the faithful swineherd of Odysseus, we have a delightful account, showing the friendliest relations between servant and master. Yet the picture is by no means too rosy. These men knew the hardships and hazards of life, the bitter nip of the night frost and the high-handed treatment of a haughty chief.

The style and habits of the chiefs recall our own medieval barons. Their life was a full and pleasant one. They were great eaters, feasting liberally on beef and pork, while slaves carved and handed round the bread in baskets. Their wine was a rich syrup which they mixed in a bowl with water before it was ladled out to the diners. Minstrels were frequently in attendance. At the feast in Alcinous' house, when the meal was over, a minstrel struck up with his harp and sang of the great deeds of famous men. '*A goodly thing it is*', Odysseus said, '*to listen to a singer such as this, like to the very gods in voice.*'

Another favourite pastime was the dance. A floor of beaten earth was specially prepared for it. Here is Homer's description of a typical scene:

> *Young squires and maids of costly dower*
> *Danced hand in hand upon the floor,*
> *These in lissom kirtles dight*
> *Those in tunics woven light,*
> *Whereon oil of olive glowed;*
> *Each maiden had a lovely crown*
> *And the young men swords of gold*
> *From silver baldrics hanging down;*
> *And whiles they tripped on cunning feet*
> *Deft moving in a reel,*
> *As when some potter at his bench*
> *Makes trial of a wheel,*
> *Fitting it between his hands,*
> *Whether it run true;*
> *And then anon in double file*
> *They danced it to and fro,*
> *And round about that lovely choir*
> *Was set a goodly throng.*
> *Full joyful were the folk to see*
> *The pleasant sight; and thereamong*
> *A holy minstrel played his harp*
> *And, as he led the tune,*
> *Two tumblers went between the ranks*
> *A-twirling up and down.*

A HOMERIC RECITER (*see opposite*)

This figure (taken from a jar the shape of which is indicated on the right) represents a man, dressed in a 'himation', from whose mouth proceed the words 'So it befell once in Tiryns'.

FIG. 7. A HOMERIC RECITER

Sometimes the dancers played a game of ball in time to the tune. Athletic exercises of a more strenuous sort were also very popular. For the Greeks were at all times great lovers of sports. At the close of Alcinous' banquet, the young men competed in running, wrestling, boxing, jumping, and weight-throwing; and Odysseus, middle aged as he was, astonished the company by throwing a monster stone 'far beyond all the other marks'.

In many of their activities the womenfolk mixed freely among the men. True, they kept their separate quarters in the house, and did not, as a rule, appear at the banquets of the males; but on the whole nothing is more remarkable than the independence of the wives and daughters of the Homeric chieftains as compared with the less enviable condition of the women of later times. The poems are full of beautiful feminine characters, such as Hector's wife Andromache, the faithful Penelope who waited twenty years for her husband's home-coming, the lovely Helen whose elopement to Troy was the prime cause of the Greeks' expedition, or the maiden Nausicaa who befriended Odysseus when washed ashore after a shipwreck.

Nothing in the Homeric poems is more remarkable than the delicacy and courtesy of the manners of this people. Young men invariably rise from their seats when an older man enters the room. Towards strangers they show an unfailing courtesy, rebuking such louts as think a foreigner fair game for insolence. The same behaviour is still to be found among the peasant folk of any European countryside, where the vulgarity of town-civilization has not yet made its way. These virtues are, it seems, common to all who live very close to nature; and certainly the Homeric folk were nothing if not natural. Their emotions were strong and honest; their loves and hates passionate. Achilles declares that, on slaying his mortal foe Hector, he could almost find it in his heart to carve and eat him raw. Women, hearing of their husbands' deaths, give themselves up to wild lament. Odysseus, when at last he meets his son after long absence, sheds tears till the going down of the sun. Yet a fine restraint is also observable in this passionate race; and perhaps this quality in them will be best understood if we close by saying a word concerning their religious beliefs.

The ancient religion of the land before the coming of the Greeks had been a gloomy worship of dark, mysterious powers which dwelt in the recesses of the Underworld and were bestial in form and cruel in temper. To placate them men made offerings of bowls of blood or even, in their despair, of human victims; and all know the story of the hideous Minotaur, half bull, half man, who lurked in the famous Labyrinth at Crete and fed on the bodies of hapless youths and maids. This sinister creed the Greeks, when they entered the land, seem in part to have adopted; for legend told how even Agamemnon, who led their host to Troy, sacrificed his own daughter Iphigeneia to win divine favour for the voyage. But, as time went on, these foul superstitions were suppressed and the creed, which the Greeks brought with them, triumphed. It was a far happier, sunnier creed. Its gods were not mysterious hobgoblins or monstrosities, but reasonable beings of human form and with the minds and passions of men. They dwelt, so it was thought, above the clouds on Mount Olympus, whose snow-capped peak rose sparkling beyond the plains of northern Thessaly. Each among them, too, had some favourite shrine in various parts of Greece: Athena at Athens, Apollo at Delphi, Zeus at Olympia. At such shrines, and at many an improvised altar too, was offered sacrifice of the thigh-bones of oxen wrapped in fat, and in many other ways. The purpose of such sacrifice was not merely to placate the gods' wrath, but to invoke their assistance in the various operations of men's daily life. Each deity had his special function. Zeus the sky-god and the wielder of the thunderbolt ruled over all Olympus and presided over the destinies of men, weighing in his golden balances their lots of life and death. Poseidon was the god of the sea and the saviour of mariners

Athena was the patroness of handicrafts; Ares the lord of war, and Apollo of healing. What therefore is specially to be noted is that the Greeks' notion of the gods was not vague and mysterious, but reasonable and clear-cut. Olympus, so to speak, was highly organized; and this sense of system was typical of the race. They liked to see everything well ordered, and they applied their *minds*, as few peoples have ever done, to the manifold problems of life. So, hot blooded and passionate as they were, they did not let their feelings run away with them. They sought to curb and direct them by the guiding restraints of reason. Above all, they disliked excess; and, if one were to choose any one of their many proverbs as peculiarly suitable for their national motto, it would be the two words inscribed over Apollo's shrine at Delphi—*Mēden agān*, 'Nothing too much'. On that principle their whole civilization was based.

But the Greeks had far to travel before they reached full civilization. For about 1100 the Heroic Age, of which we have been speaking, came abruptly to an end. In the wake of the Achaeans came other migratory tribes of Greek-speaking peoples. They were called the Dorians and, unlike their Achaean predecessors, they were too rough and barbarous to appreciate the culture which they found in the lands they conquered. They sacked the lordly palaces of Tiryns and Mycenae. All the arts and riches laboriously built up through many centuries were thus suddenly swept away; and a Dark Age followed. But the germ of the Greek genius was working. Order was at last evolved out of chaos; and after four or five centuries of semi-barbarism a new and even more brilliant culture was to blossom forth among the city-states of what we call historic Greece.

II

THE CITY-STATE

THE landscape of Greece was worthy of its people. Modern travellers who journey thither intending to visit its museums and admire its temples find themselves to their own surprise entranced by the natural beauty of its scenery. Everywhere are mountains—more naked and barren perhaps than in anti-quity, since pine forests and oak coppices were used up long ago for ships' timbers and other purposes—yet even in the old days the fine sharp outline of the hills must have stood out strong and clear in the crystal atmosphere of Mediterranean sunshine. Shallow scrub covers their lower slopes; and among the scrub lies such a litter of boulders and loose shale that some agility is needed in picking one's way among them, and path-ways normally follow the course of some dry ravine or torrent-bed. Between the ranges of these hills lie narrow level strips of fertile plain-land, brilliant in spring-time with the emerald green of young corn crops in vivid contrast to the shimmering grey of the extensive olive orchards. Towards the foot of the plain the vista between the pale blue mountains broadens out, dis-closing a horizon of the deep blue sea, calm as a lake in summer, sparkling with the 'myriad laughter' of tiny dancing wavelets and strewn with the grey shapes of countless rocky islets.[1]

It was in such plains—and there are many—that the Greeks, when first they arrived out of the north, settled down to make their homes. For some centuries they lived, as they had settled, in scattered villages or groups of villages, each under its local chief. Then bit by bit the groups began to league themselves together, for common religious celebrations, a common market, and common defence; but, most important of all, for common government. Thus in each plain there came to be formed a

[1] See bird's-eye view on p. 21.

separate political community; and the need arising for some political centre, its members chose some convenient hill-top which would serve equally for fortress and for capital. The name which the Greeks gave to such a fortress-capital was Polis or City; and the community of plain-dwellers who united in a common allegiance to this central Polis[1] is known as a City-State.

Now these city-states were something entirely novel in the history of the world. Other ancient peoples—the inhabitants of Mesopotamia,[2] for example, or the Egyptians—dwelt in plains of enormous area and their millions were content to obey the despotic rule of hereditary kings. Not so the Greeks; for their city-states were so diminutive and the citizens lived so close to the centre of government that they soon grew dissatisfied with the blundering of their monarchs. So one after another these monarchies were suppressed; and the members of each city-state undertook the adventurous task of governing themselves. To find oneself master of one's own destiny is a thrilling experience, as every young man knows when he emerges from the restraints of school or home; and the Greeks, enjoying the taste of political responsibility, were fiercely proud of their freedom. They were fired by an intensity of local patriotism which is difficult for us to imagine. To say that they loved their Polis is far short of the mark. She was all in all to them; and to be banished from her confines was a calamity almost worse than death itself. They were prepared to die for her; and wars

[1] It is easy to see how much Greek ideas of government have influenced later ages; for many of our words such as 'Politics', 'Politician', &c., are derived from this old Greek word for the state.

[2] The recently discovered civilization of the Sumerians, however, affords a parallel to the city-state.

ARCADIA (*see opposite*)

Typical mountain scenery showing the boulder-strown hill-side, olive-trees, and in the foreground the ruins of a temple.

FIG. 8. ARCADIA

C

between city-state and city-state were unhappily so frequent and so bitter that the common unity of the Greek race as a whole was often lost completely from sight; and in the end the country was ruined by long-drawn internal strife. Such was the heavy price which Greece was forced to pay for this division into small political units—the largest of which did not exceed the area of a middle-sized English county. Yet the division was worth while; for only on so small a scale could the experiment of self-government have been attempted; and it produced, as we shall see, the most astonishing results.

By the end of the seventh century B.C. there had been formed many scores of such diminutive city-states not merely on the Greek mainland itself, but on the Aegean Islands and along the western coast of Asia Minor. Nor was this all; for the growth of population induced many states to send out colonists; and thus sprang up on the surrounding coasts of Sicily, Italy, and elsewhere a further crop of similar communities, almost completely independent of the mother-state who sent them out, and governing themselves according to the selfsame methods as they had known at home.

At first it was not *all* the inhabitants of a city-state who could claim a share of political privilege. The conditions of life were still mainly agricultural; many of the folk were little better than serfs; and the larger landowners monopolized political power, making the laws, delivering judgement on disputes, and deciding the issues of peace and war. Self-government therefore meant government by the wealthier class only. Oligarchy or the Rule of the Few is the name given to such government; and at the close of the seventh century oligarchies were general among the city-states of Greece.

Henceforward it will be well to concentrate our attention on two of these states, Sparta and Athens. About these far more is known; and the contrast between their political institutions adds special point to their choice.

III

LIFE AT SPARTA

I. THE LYCURGAN SYSTEM

AMONG the many city-states of Greece one of the most interesting was Sparta. This state had been formed in the beautiful valley of Lacedaemon in the south of the Peloponnese. It is a pleasant land, rich with trees and crops, well watered by the river Eurotas and other streams which flow down from the great mountain Taygetus upon its western side. The tribe of conquering Dorians, who had occupied it, had enslaved the original inhabitants, making them till the soil as serfs or *Helots*. By and by they crossed Mount Taygetus and, conquering the adjacent plain of Messenia, made serfs of its inhabitants too. Now the Spartans themselves were not very numerous, not more than a few thousand at most; and the serfs or Helots outnumbered them by ten or twenty to one. This was a dangerous situation; and about the middle of the seventh century the Helots suddenly rose in revolt. By a tremendous effort the Spartans at length wore the rebels down. But they had learnt their lesson. They were determined never to risk a repetition of the awful crisis. So a couple of generations later they undertook a complete reorganization of their national life.[1]

The authorship of this celebrated reform was attributed by tradition to a certain Lycurgus; and, though of Lycurgus himself we have no reliable information, the character and

---

[1] The constitution of Sparta comprised all three political elements which were present in the primitive community of Homeric times. These were: two hereditary *Kings* whose functions were eventually confined to commanding the army in war; a *Council of Elders* called the *Gerousia*: an *Assembly of Citizens* who were allowed little real voice in policy, their verdict being ascertained by the crude method of seeing whether 'Ayes' or 'Noes' shouted the louder. Besides these three, however, and, as time went on, developing more importance than them all, was a body of five *Ephors* who were annually elected and who in reality directed the affairs of the state.

object of the reform is well known to us. It sought by an iron discipline to train the entire body of Spartan citizens into an efficient garrison for the suppression of the serfs.

The Lycurgan system began with the upbringing of the young. At birth a male Spartan was inspected by the elders. If weakly, they ordered him to be exposed on the mountain-side and left to die. If likely to grow up to be a serviceable soldier, he was permitted to live and left for the first seven years in the charge of his mother. The women of Sparta were famous for their stalwart limbs and stout hearts. Where public interests were concerned, they did not flinch from any sacrifice. 'Return *with* your shield or *on* it' was the advice they gave when their sons went forth to war, implying that to be borne home wounded was preferable to the loss of shield in ignominious flight. Some mothers were even known to kill their sons for cowardice. Compared with the women of the rest of Greece, they enjoyed considerable independence; and as nurses they were everywhere much in request.

At seven home-life ended, and the boy was drafted into a sort of boarding-school with sixty or more others. The super-intendent was an older man with a youth of twenty to assist him, to say nothing of attendants called 'Floggers'. Some of the leading boys were given the position of prefects and allowed to 'fag' the rest. All lived and fed together in a common mess; and it was a part of their training that the boys should supplement their scanty rations by stealing off the neighbouring farms. This practice was intended to develop resourcefulness and courage; and there is a famous story of a lad who, being caught in the act of stealing a tame fox, hid the animal under his cloak

---

VALE OF SPARTA (*see opposite*)

Above the plain rich with fruit-trees and tillage rise the cliffs and snowclad peaks of Mount Taygetus, across which lies the mountain track to the Messenian Plain.

Fig. 9. VALE OF SPARTA

and allowed it to lacerate his vitals rather than accept the disgrace of exposure.

Toughness was, indeed, the principal quality which the Lycurgan system aimed at producing. The boys went barefoot, wore but a single garment, and lay on a bed of thistledown and reeds. They swam in the Eurotas, one of the few strong-flowing rivers of Greece, drawing its waters from the snow-capped peaks of Mount Taygetus which towers above the Vale of Lacedaemon. All manner of sports were practised, running, wrestling, quoit-throwing, and above all dancing, which resembled what we should call musical drill. There were games specially devised to promote pugnacity. In one the lads were divided into two teams or packs; and one team being posted on an island surrounded by streams, it was the business of the other team to expel them by main force, kicking, biting, scratching and even tearing at each others' eyes.

As for school-lessons, as we ourselves know them, there were very few. It is doubtful how far the majority were even taught to read or write. Memory was trained by learning the laws of the state by heart; and most could recite some Homer and the favourite songs of their patriot-poet Tyrtaeus. Rhetoric, or the art of public speaking[1] which other Greeks so much admired, the Spartans despised and mistrusted. They even affected a deliberate curtness of speech of which many examples might be given. 'Breakfast here, supper in Hades', said one of their generals when his army was hopelessly entrapped. Once a foreign ambassador, who came to Sparta seeking assistance, addressed a long harangue to the councillors, who at its conclusion remarked that they had forgotten the first half and could not follow the second. Next day he took the hint and, producing a sack, simply said 'Sack wants flour'. 'You might have left out "sack"' was the answer. As this story shows, these taciturn folk were

---

[1] Here again our own word 'rhetoric' is derived from the Greek word *rhētor*, a public speaker.

Fig. 10. MUSICAL DRILL (A PYRRHIC DANCE)

not without a certain shrewdness and a dry sense of humour; and even to-day we sometimes speak of a terse, pithy saying as 'laconic', that is like 'Lacedaemonian' speech. But their woful illiteracy stunted their development. They produced no art and no literature of real merit. They were incapable of large views; and though Sparta might have played a glorious part as the leader of the whole Greek race, her history is one long tale of lost opportunities.

At the same time we must remember that the Spartans' over-emphasis on physical exercise had a definite purpose—the making of good soldiers. No sport likely to overdevelop the wrong muscles or otherwise injure the growth of the body was permitted; and for this reason boxing wás banned. Once every ten days the boys underwent an official inspection. Their physique was superb. It is unlikely that there was ever a finer race.

Boyhood over, a citizen's first taste of practical duties began and it was a grim one. At eighteen he was drafted into the Secret Corps or Crypteia; and for two years it was his business to go forth among the Helot population of the countryside and, searching out the more dangerous characters among them, to make away with these in as secret a manner as possible. Once as many as two thousand Helots were thus dispatched at a single time and nobody knew how.

Manhood brought no release from the stern discipline of the Lycurgan system. Communal life was in fact the keynote of the Spartans' whole existence. Though hard, it had many compensations. Drill was a regular part of their daily routine; but, like all true soldiers, they enjoyed the zest of team-work and organized co-operation. They liked to feel themselves, as rowers do, a part of an efficient machine; and the spirit of comradeship, which this engendered, was not confined to the parade-ground. It entered into every department of their daily habits. All full-grown citizens lived, like the boys, a barrack-life

FIG. 11. A RUNNER

This man is in the attitude of starting for the 'Hoplite Race'; on his head is
a helmet the crest of which is missing; as also is the shield that should be
on his arm.

in messes called Syssitia. Their quarters were kept deliberately simple. No decoration was permitted, the law forbidding the use of any tool except the axe. Clothing too was of the simplest; and the foul condition of a Spartan's garments was notorious. They were far from being a cleanly race. In the messes the fare consisted chiefly of pork, cheese, figs, bread, and wine. Spartan broth was famous for its nastiness, so that one stranger declared on tasting it that he now understood why no Spartan feared death. Hunting might add to the menu; but normally each individual member was required to make a monthly contribution of food to the common table. This was provided by the Helots from his farm. No citizen ever worked the land himself.

Even trading was forbidden him, but was left to a class, neither citizens nor serfs, who lived in districts more or less distant from the capital. Thus the amassing of wealth was deliberately discouraged; for it was held that, so long as the citizens possessed no personal interests, they would remain the more devoted servants of the common weal. Money-making indeed was rendered almost impossible, since the only coinage recognized at Sparta was a currency of heavy iron spits. A sum sufficient to purchase a slave would have filled a good-sized wagon!

So stern was the discipline that little scope was left for personal responsibility; and, just as the boys had always a grown man hanging round their heels to keep them out of mischief, so even the Spartan commanders-in-chief were often hampered by the presence of government spies. The result was unfortunate; for when Spartans went abroad and passed beyond the control of the home authorities, they often took to drink and self-indulgence. For they had never learned the true habit of self-mastery for lack of genuine opportunity at home. Nevertheless so long as they were in guiding-strings, they remained the most devoted servants of the state, and their iron discipline made them magnificent soldiers. Their abundant leisure too allowed daily opportunity for drill; and to appreciate the importance of such training in the military history of Greece, it will be well to say something here about Greek methods of fighting.

II. METHODS OF GREEK WARFARE

Since Homeric times these methods had undergone a change. Combats between single champions had gone out of fashion. They were replaced by the charge of a well-ordered battle-line of heavy-armed warriors or hoplites. These fought at close quarters, using not the old missile javelin, but a six-foot thrusting lance.[1] Their defensive equipment, on the other hand, was much the same as before—a helmet, cuirass, greaves, and a large oval shield which covered the whole body from chin to knee. Thus equipped, they presented to the enemy a front well protected from head to foot. The battle-line or phalanx was formed of a solid rectangle of such hoplites, ranged eight ranks deep as a rule and marching side by side in such close formation that each man was partially covered by his neighbour's shield. So long as the line held firm, its front was almost impenetrable. The two opposed armies, charging against each other to the tune of the pipe, met with a crash which on one occasion, we are told, could be heard at some miles' distance. There then ensued a struggle that more than anything else resembled a football scrum, in which the combatants stood upright and, pushing with their shields and thrusting with their spears, strove to heave their opponents back. So long as the shield-line held, it was difficult even for spears to penetrate the hoplite's armour; but once it broke it was a different matter. Taken in flank or rear, his cuirass offered no adequate protection to the lower portions of his body; and if he fled, casting his cumbrous shield aside, he could be hunted down and dispatched

[1] A short sword was also carried at the side for use at close quarters.

with ease. For this reason the casualties of a defeated army were often out of all proportion to the victors' losses.

For armies thus heavily accoutred and closely marshalled, the first essential was smooth ground for manœuvre. On the broken boulder-strewn hill-side the hoplite would flounder hopelessly. So most battles were fought on the plain; and it was only on occasions when some wild mountain tribe was the enemy that light-armed troops, armed with bows and slings, played a really important part.[1] Cavalry, too, were little used; for the plains of southern Greece were too small to afford easy manœuvre, and only in the wide plains of Thessaly in the north did horse-breeding and horsemanship attain much vogue.

The Greeks clung to the traditional methods of fighting almost as though to the rules of a game. Occasionally, it is true, the rules were broken, and with surprising success. Once a Spartan general, instead of accepting the enemy's challenge when they drew up in regular battle-order, deliberately waited until the 'fall-out' order was given, and then fell on them seated at dinner and wiped them all out. Sometimes an enemy would refuse battle altogether and skulk behind his town-walls (for all cities were fortified except Sparta, where the constant presence of the Helots would have made even such a precaution useless). In these circumstances the invader might attempt (though this was rare) to force an entrance to the city. Sometimes battering-rams were employed to breach the walls. We hear, too, of an ingenious engine consisting of a nozzle attached to a furnace through which flames were blown by bellows on to the inflammable parts of the defences. Sometimes, too, a mound was piled against the wall to facilitate an entry; and the defenders, to meet this, would tunnel underground, drawing the earth

---

[1] In the fourth century B.C., when other states besides the Spartans began to train professional armies, light-armed troops were drilled in tactics which proved highly successful against the hitherto invincible hoplites. Another equally successful innovation was the massing of the hoplite ranks to a depth of twenty or even fifty deep against the normal eight.

FIG. 12. A HOPLITE

The spear from his right hand is missing; otherwise his armour is complete—crested helmet with cheek-pieces, metal cuirass to waist, greaves on lower legs, and shield covering upper legs and body.

away below as fast as more earth was piled above. Failing success by such methods, the besiegers might settle down to a regular blockade, building a wall completely round the city to check sorties and cut off supplies. It was not unusual to add a second wall outside the first to counter any attempt at relief; and the space between the two walls might be roofed over to afford comfortable quarters if the siege ran on through winter.

Normally, however, an invading army would endeavour to provoke a reluctant enemy to battle by ravaging his lands, destroying crops, felling trees, and setting farms ablaze. In days when most states were self-supporting, a people's harvest was its most vulnerable point. This fact, moreover, had its effect on the attackers too. For they equally depended on getting in their crops; and, as open warfare was unfashionable in winter months, the spring-time campaigns were for the most part brief, the soldier-citizens being impatient to get back home for their reaping in May or June. For in nearly all the states of Greece the army was composed of men called up from plough or workshop when the outbreak of a war demanded it. The Spartans alone possessed a standing army of what may be called professional soldiers; and the fact that they spent their lives in the continual practice of arms gave them an immense superiority over the half-trained militia of their neighbours. For under the conditions of warfare which we have described above it is obvious that victory was bound to go to the army best drilled to keep its ranks and move in perfect unison.

So for two centuries and more the Spartans proved victorious on nearly every battle-field; and as a result they gained the supremacy over almost all the states of the Peloponnese. Not indeed that they were popular. Their dour, brutal character and their selfish inability to understand the feelings of other folk gave them an ill name for high-handed tyranny. On the other hand, no true Greek could withhold his admiration for their superb physical development, their dogged courage, and their self-sacrificing devotion to their own country's cause. So even beyond the Peloponnese the Spartans were respected as well as feared; and happily, when it came to the test, they were found ready to use their supremacy for more worthy ends than selfish aggrandizement. At a moment of awful peril, when the whole country was threatened by a barbarian invader, they came forward as champions of the Greek national cause.

In 480 B.C. Xerxes, King of Persia, led an enormous expedition into Greece with intent to add the country to his already vast domains.

All the country north of the Isthmus was overrun. Then two decisive battles were fought. First, in the Straits of Salamis the ships of the Greeks, and especially of the Athenians, utterly defeated the great Persian fleet. Xerxes fled for home; but he left a land-army to complete the subjugation of the northern half of the peninsula. In 479 a Greek host, led by the Spartans, overwhelmed this army at Plataea in Boeotia. It was an amazing triumph, for Persia was the strongest power in the world. The Greeks were uplifted by a new sense of their national greatness. They realized more than ever before the true value of liberty. The prestige of Sparta had never stood so high.

IV

THE RISE OF ATHENS

WHILE the Spartans were making good their domination of the Peloponnese, Athens had been striking out along different lines. At first she was a purely agricultural state, poor and insignificant. Then during the sixth century B.C. industries had been started, especially the manufacture of pottery for export. Foreign traders had come to settle. A promising trade had been begun; and shortly before the Persian invasion the discovery of rich silver ore in south-east Attica had been utilized to build the

Fig. 13. Bird's-eye view of Ancient Athens from N.E.

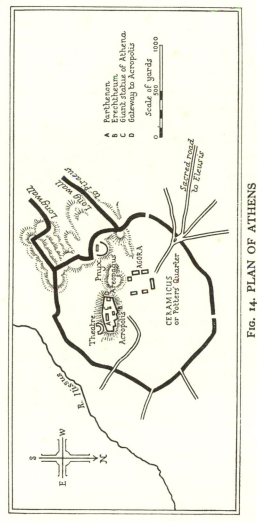

FIG. 14. PLAN OF ATHENS

VIEW OF ATHENS SEEN FROM N.E. (*see opposite*)

On the distant sea-horizon lies the Island of Aegina and beyond it the mountains of the Peloponnese. On the sea-coast to the right lies the Piraeus harbour with the line of the Long Walls leading to it. On the Acropolis may be seen

(A) the Parthenon, (B) to the right front of the Parthenon another smaller temple, the Erechtheum, (C) to the right of the Erechtheum the colossal bronze statue of Athena, (D) to the right of this the Entrance Gate or Propylaea.

The spur at the foot of the right or western end of the Acropolis is the Areopagus or Hill of Ares; and on the low hills to the right of this again is the Pnyx or open-air theatre of debate. [N.B. The dramatic theatre of Dionysus is out of sight on the farther slope of the Acropolis facing the sea.] In the town itself the market-place lies at the foot of the Acropolis and Areopagus; from the market-place an avenue of trees leads to the Dipylon Gate through which ran the Sacred road to Eleusis.

powerful fleet which helped to win the Battle of Salamis. Along with this economic development, too, had come an important political change. Artisans and traders are usually less conservative than agricultural peasants; and the growing population of Athens had asserted their independence against the nobility of landowners. They had established a real democracy in which the Many, not the Few, were to control the government.

This change, together with the national enthusiasm at the victory over Persia, bred a new spirit of enterprise and adventure in the Athenians. Soon this new spirit found scope. Across the Aegean many Greek towns and islands of the Asia Minor coast had recently fallen under Persian rule. Seeing the Persians defeated in Greece, these towns were eager to throw off the hated yoke: and they appealed to Sparta for aid. Sparta with characteristic caution hung back. But Athens accepted the role of leadership and threw all her energy into the crusade of liberation. Under the protection of her fleet was formed a confederacy of Greek maritime states. It had its centre at Delos and was called the Delian League. Its efforts were successful; and the Persians' attempts to recover their hold were frustrated. Then, feeling secure once more, many members of the League felt that its purpose was finished. But Athens thought otherwise; and one by one, as they tried to break away, she overcame them and reduced them to a state of subjection to herself. So Athens from being the leader of a voluntary confederacy became the mistress of an empire.

The final step in the transformation was taken when in 454 the common fund of the League was moved from the Treasury at Delos to the Acropolis or Citadel of Athens. The author of this high-handed act was Pericles, the great statesman who in the middle of the fifth century attained a commanding position in Athenian politics. Though constitutionally elected to office year by year, he made himself by sheer force of character the virtual dictator of Athens and for thirty years he maintained his unique authority as the leader and guide of her young democracy.

Under Pericles' administration the power of the city went from strength to strength. The subjects of her Empire were ruled with a firm hand. The fund formed from the tax which they still paid into her treasury accumulated steadily. Throughout the Aegean trade flourished under the protection of her all-powerful fleet. The population multiplied. Foreigners came to settle; and the city grew rich as no other Greek city had been rich before. Above all, the artistic and literary genius of its members was developed to a pitch unrivalled in the history of the world. For Pericles was an enthusiastic patron of the arts. He built temples which were supreme masterpieces of architecture. He gathered round him a company of sculptors, poets, historians, and thinkers whose names must rank among the greatest of all time. In a word, he made Athens, as he himself boasted, an 'education to Greece'.

In culture, therefore, as in power, Athens now far outshone her sister-states of Greece; and partly for this reason, partly because from such portions of her literature as still survive we can know more of her than of the other states, it will be well henceforward to concentrate almost exclusively upon the various aspects of Athenian life. Broadly speaking, though other states lagged far behind the brilliance of Athens' democracy, we may take what is said about her ways and customs as more or less typical of the rest.

V

ATHENIAN DEMOCRACY

I. POLITICS

In these days of huge national states whose population is numbered by the million and of empires which extend over many continents, it is very difficult to form a clear idea of what democracy meant in a Greek city-state. We call England a democracy; but in point of fact the political activities and interests of the average Englishman are very limited. He casts a vote at parliamentary elections once in every five years. Perhaps he reads the newspaper summaries of parliamentary debates at times of particular crisis. It is hard, in short, for the average

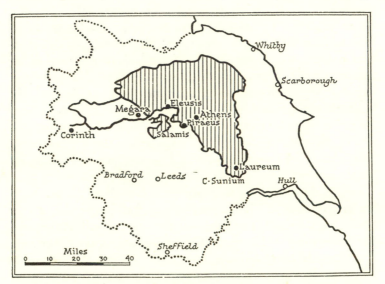

FIG. 15. MAP OF ATTICA, PLACED FOR COMPARISON IN YORKSHIRE

man to believe that he has very much to do with what goes on at Westminster.

But in Athens it was far otherwise. There any decision that was taken was apt to have an instantaneous and profound effect on the citizen's daily life; and, what was more important still, every citizen had a direct share in the making of those decisions For every adult male—unless he were a slave or a foreigner residing in Athens—was entitled to vote in the general Assembly or Ecclesia; and in all matters of importance the Assembly of citizens had the final say. It is as though the management of a school was controlled not by the head master or a body of governors, but by a Debating Society consisting of the pupils themselves. We can easily picture with what interest and enthusiasm such a Debating Society's meetings and proceedings would be followed by every member of the school.

So, when an Assembly met at Athens (as it did at stated intervals), a considerable proportion of the citizens would be there. Outlying farmers might find it difficult to attend: but residents in the capital were expected to be present; and loungers were swept out of the market-place by a rope well drenched in vermilion. A stain of red on a man's cloak meant a fine; for the Athenians did not hold with the shirking of public duties.

The meeting took place soon after dawn, and was held in a sort of rude open-air theatre upon a sloping hill-side called the Pnyx. A herald ordained silence. Prayers were offered by a priest and a black pig was sacrificed. For superstition still played a large part even in political ceremonies; and if an earthquake shock were felt or a drop of rain fell, the bad omen was considered sufficient cause for adjourning the meeting. A committee of the Council (of which more shall be said) presided over the debate, and when they had taken their places business began.

'Who wishes to speak?' cried the herald; and whoever was for addressing the meeting mounted a platform hewn from the rock. Speeches were followed with eager attention, the audience shouting applause or booing and hissing in displeasure. The officials of the state took, of course, a leading part in the debates. After Pericles' death demagogues arose—men of low birth and still lower principles who appealed to the worst instincts of the mob. One named Cleon was notorious for his vulgar and violent behaviour on the platform. He ranted, strode about, waved his arms, bared his leg and slapped his thigh in a most undignified manner. From the historian Thucydides we have a vivid picture of this man's first political triumph. Athens was at war with

Sparta at the time; and her fleet had succeeded in isolating a detachment of enemy troops on the island of Sphacteria. But her commanders had utterly failed to push home their advantage. *'Cleon sarcastically declared that, if the generals were good for anything, they might easily capture the men and that, were he himself a general, he would certainly do so. . . . Nicias (who was one of the generals) replied that, so far as they were concerned, he might take what forces he wanted and make the attempt. Fancying Nicias' offer to be mere pretence, Cleon at first was quite willing to go, but when he perceived that it was made in good earnest, he tried to back out, saying that Nicias and not he was general. . . . But the more Cleon declined the proffered command, so much the more did the mob, as their manner is, urge Nicias to resign and shout to Cleon to sail. At length, not knowing how to escape from his own rash words, Cleon undertook the expedition and pledged his word that within twenty days he would either bring back the Spartans prisoner or kill them on the spot. . . . His vain boast moved the Athenians to laughter; but the wiser sort reflected with glee that of two good things one was certain—either there would be an end of Cleon, which they greatly preferred, or else he would put the Spartans into their hands.'*

Actually Cleon made good his astonishing boast. But demagogues were not always as shrewd or so successful as he; and Athens paid dearly for the readiness of the mob to throw over the more trusty commanders at the bidding of low-mouthed agitators.[1]

Attendance at Assembly was only one side of a citizen's political activities. In many other ways he might take a part in the government of his country. For in another respect an Athenian's notion of politics was very different from our own. Nowadays, for the most part, we are ruled by officials paid and retained by the state—civil servants, judges, tax-collectors,

---

[1] Voting was sometimes ascertained by a deliberate count, but usually by a show of hands.

inspectors of education, health-officers, and other salaried experts. Now, with their passion for freedom, the democratic Athenians were loth to trust power in the hands of such permanent officials. They preferred to leave the administration to ordinary citizens who at the end of their year's office would retire again into private life and let other ordinary citizens take their place. So all public posts were filled by unpaid volunteers; and first and last a man might serve the state in many different capacities.

First, in his own 'deme' or parish there would be many minor jobs to be done; and in these a public-spirited citizen might serve his political apprenticeship. Next, he might aspire to election to the central State-Council of five hundred members which carried on current business while the Assembly was not sitting and prepared the motions for the Assembly's discussion. At the Assembly's meetings a committee of the Council presided, the councillors taking it in turns to act chairman for the day; so one fine morning our friend might find himself in this responsible position and for a proud twenty-four hours might hold the Treasury keys in his keeping.

If he were more ambitious still, our public-spirited friend might stand for the office of archon at the annual election, and, if successful, might preside over trials in the law courts or superintend the religious ceremonial of the state. Finally, he might even be elected a general, which in peace time would give him wide powers of financial administration and, in war, the command of an army or fleet. But, whereas the lesser officials, such as archons and councillors, were selected *by lot* from men chosen by the local constituencies, the generals were elected by a direct vote of the people; so that, as a rule, only men of influence or tried capacity could rise to this supreme position. Nevertheless, persons of humble origin sometimes made their way to the top. Cleon was a leather-merchant; and another successful upstart was a maker of lyres. So far did the

Athenians go in their preference for the amateur rather than the professional man.

Meanwhile, besides a large variety of other posts—market-inspectors, dock-superintendents, and so forth—which occupied a considerable number of citizens, there was one further capacity in which the richer folk at any rate might serve the state. Taxation was no more popular at Athens than elsewhere. But since there were no salaried posts, the requirements of the Exchequer were normally met by the proceeds of harbour-dues and legal fines, to say nothing of the revenue from silver-mines or the tribute paid by the allies. For certain purposes, however, it was found desirable to call on the wealthier citizens to put their hands in their pockets. The equipment of state galleys, for instance, and the production of plays at the annual dramatic competitions were financed in this manner. Names were taken from the lists in rotation. A man could, if he chose, evade his responsibility by proving some one else to be wealthier than himself. But, as a rule, he would take a pride in performing his duty. In the production of plays there was the keenest possible rivalry in providing the richest costumes and training the most efficient chorus. If his play proved successful in the competition, a man would even put up some monument in the public streets to commemorate his victory.

II. THE LAW COURTS

Extraordinary as it may appear, the preservation of order at Athens was entrusted not to citizens but to foreigners—and foreign slaves at that. For the idea of one citizen acting policeman over another was utterly distasteful. So the state employed a corps of barbarian archers, drawn from the Scythian tribesmen of the north and clad in their native trousers and high-peaked, tight-fitting caps. They lived in tents not far from the Acropolis, or Citadel.

Even in the administration of justice the same dislike of

officialdom prevailed. There was no such thing as a public prosecutor at Athens. It was left to private individuals to prosecute even in cases of theft, murder, high treason, and other crimes against society. Various forms of procedure were, of course, employed according to the nature of the crime. Homicide was dealt with by a special court of elders which sat on the Areopagus, or 'Hill of Ares', mentioned under its Latin name in the Biblical account of St. Paul's visit to the city. Criminal cases were treated in a different fashion from civil disputes about property or contracts. But it was always left to some individual citizen to take the first step. He would begin by serving a summons on the offender in the presence of witnesses. Then after an interval the two would appear before a magistrate; and a preliminary hearing of the case would take place. At this hearing evidence would be taken down by a clerk. The testimony of slaves was always elicited under torture, on the assumption that only so could they be trusted to tell the truth against their master. Copies of laws and other documents might be produced; and when all the relevant material was complete, it was put in a box and sealed up.

After another interval, the trial proper took place before a jury. A magistrate presided, but the verdict was left entirely to a body of citizen-jurors. To the quick-witted Athenians the chance of hearing a good piece of rhetorical argument was a form of intellectual entertainment. There was therefore no disinclination to serve on the panel. Moreover, jurors were paid a small fee for their trouble; and a large number of candidates, drawn mainly from the elderly or unemployed, were always waiting round the court doors in the morning. The size of the juries was large—numbering 201, 401, or sometimes even more. Until the day of the trial none knew who would serve; bribery was out of the question.

The court was in the open air. It contained benches for jurors and a platform for speakers. The witnesses would be in attendance, but only to attest the accuracy of their statements, a copy of which was produced from the sealed box and read aloud. There was no regular cross-examination. Each party made a long speech, a time-limit being set by a water-clock which worked on the same principle as a sand-glass. No professional pleaders were allowed, and the litigants were compelled to address the court in person. There was, however, nothing to prevent the inexperienced from getting a practised speech-writer to compose a speech for them. This was frequently done, and numerous samples still survive. Many dealt with disputes about property or contracts. We have one speech concerned with a quarrel over a certain plot of ground which one man declared to be part of his orchard, and the other to be a watercourse running down a public footpath. Another speech, written for a young man who complained of assault and battery, gives us a vivid picture of Athenian 'horse-play'. First he is careful to explain the origin of his feud with the defendants—how, when he was doing his two years' service with the army, they had bullied him disgracefully, '*falling upon him, beating him, and emptying the slops over him*', till '*such was the uproar round the tent that the general and other officers rushed out in the nick of time to prevent serious damage being done*'. Next he describes how, when back in Athens, these desperate fellows had reeled out one evening from a bout of heavy drinking and encountering him in the street had '*stripped him of his cloak, tripped him up, rolled him in the mud, and jumped on him to such effect that his lip was cut and his eye bunged up*', and finally, one of them mounted on the body of his prostrate victim, '*crowing like a cock and flapping his arms against his sides in imitation of wings*'. After much long-winded argument the speech concludes with a contrast between the scandalous lives led by the alleged assailants and the exemplary character of the young man himself. Arguments were employed which would never be admitted in an English law-court. Politics were dragged in on the least opportunity. Appeals for pity were frequent; and sometimes the accused would parade his children in rags and claim indulgence on the score of domestic responsibilities. The jurymen were clearly susceptible to such emotional appeals. They expressed their feelings by shouts, stamping, and groans. Sometimes speakers were forced to protest against the frequent

FIG. 16. JUROR'S TICKET AND OBOL

The ticket is inscribed with the juror's name, Epicrates, and his 'deme' or parish, Skabo. He would receive as his day's pay three tiny silver *obols* of which front and back is here shown

interruptions. Nevertheless, verdicts would seem to have been tolerably fair. Juries may have had little accurate knowledge of the niceties of law; but they were shrewd judges of their neighbour's character and could distinguish the honest man from the knave. We know that the Athenian courts were famous for the high standard of justice.

The voting was by ballot. Each juror was provided with a mussel-shell which at the close of the trial he placed in one or other of two jars, for condemnation or acquittal. If the penalty was not defined by statute, conviction was followed by a second vote on the nature of the sentence. Either side could propose a penalty. The jury then decided between their suggestions by a second vote.

The penalties under Athenian law varied between fines,

disfranchisement, exile, and death. Imprisonment was not favoured; for there was no adequate provision for keeping men long in jail, and in all probability sentiment was against it. Those under condemnation of death were sometimes kept under lock and key for a while. The method of execution was merciful. The condemned man drank a dose of hemlock which caused gradual paralysis of the limbs till death supervened.

III. MILITARY AND NAVAL DUTIES

No picture of an Athenian citizen's public responsibilities would be complete without some allusion to his military duties. It was, of course, the rule of every Greek city-state that its inhabitants might be called upon to bear arms. Wars were frequent; and at the end of Pericles' lifetime the antagonism of Athens and Sparta brought on a war which lasted on and off for twenty-seven years.[1] Thus most of the Athenian citizen-body were engaged at frequent intervals in one form or another of war service.

At eighteen, on coming of age, a young man was enrolled in a corps known as the Epheboi, and for two years underwent his military training. At enrolment, he would swear an oath of loyalty to the state: '*I will not disgrace my sacred weapons nor desert the comrade at my side. I will fight for things holy and things profane, whether I am alone or with others. I will hand on my fatherland greater and better than I found it. I will hearken to the magistrates and obey the existing laws and those hereafter established by the people. . . . I will honour the temples and the religion which my forefathers established. So help me Aglauros,*

---

[1] This war is known as the Peloponnesian War.

EPHEBE'S GRAVE (*see opposite*)

This vase-painting shows the gravestone of a youth; who, clad in Ephebe's cloak or 'chlamys', is represented as standing by his own tomb on which a girl is placing offerings from a basket.

Fig. 17. EPHEBE'S GRAVE

Enyalios, Ares, Zeus, Thallo, Auxo, Hegemone.' The Ephebe
would wear a uniform called the chlamys—a cloak which hung
down in pointed ends both back and front. During the second
year of training he would be quartered in a garrison fort on the
frontier of Attica. Thereafter, up to his sixtieth year, he would
remain liable to service; and if mobilization orders were posted
in the market-place, would take down his shield from among the
rafters, provide himself with rations of salt fish, onions, and
garlic, and line up in the ranks of the citizen-army. The test
would be severe for a middle-aged man. One author gives us a
comical picture of a wheezy, flabby-fleshed tradesman who
found it hard to keep the pace with his fellows. It is easy to
understand why the Athenians attached such importance to
athletics.

Even apart from her wars against neighbouring city-states,
Athens, as the head of an Empire, often found herself engaged
farther afield. It is an extraordinary testimony to the energy
of her citizens that they could support the many burdens which
her bold policy placed upon them. There is in a Paris museum
a stone, unearthed in Attica, bearing the following inscription:
*'Of the Erechtheid tribe these were they that died in the wars, in
Cyprus, in Egypt, in Phoenice, at Halieis, at Megara, in the same
year.'* A tribe represented one-tenth of a population which
cannot have exceeded 50,000 adult males.

Land warfare, however, was not the strong point of the
Athenians. Nor was there need that it should be. The city
itself was strongly fortified; and a pair of high walls, five miles
in length, had been built connecting its fortifications with the
port. Thus secure of getting their supplies by sea, the inhabitants
could defy all attempt at a siege; and there was no call to run

---

SHIPS RACING (*see opposite*)

Note the mainsails bellying to the wind, the two stern-paddles used for
steering, the beaks shaped like a fish's snout.

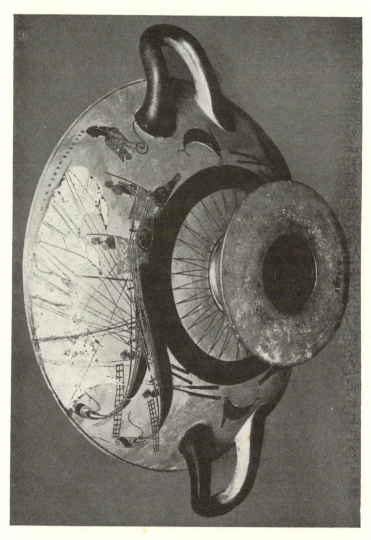

Fig. 18. SHIPS RACING

the risk of a pitched battle. So when, towards the end of the fifth century, Athens embarked upon her lengthy war with Sparta, all the population of Attica gathered into the shelter of the city; and the Spartans were left to wreak what havoc they chose upon the crops and farmsteads. Such depredations, however unpleasant, could make no impression upon the impregnable city; and, so long as the Athenians remained masters of the sea, they retained the upper hand. Furthermore, they depended not merely for their supplies, but also for their financial resources, upon the maintenance of their maritime empire. The upkeep of their fleet was therefore the primary concern of the Athenian people; and the finding of its crews the severest strain upon their strictly limited man power.

IV. NAVAL WARFARE

An ancient galley (or trireme, as it was called) was fitted with a mast which carried a large mainsail for running before the wind. Otherwise it depended on rowing. The oarsmen sat underdeck in the hold, but how they were arranged is something of a mystery. The most likely theory is that they sat in groups of threes, the oars of each group working against three tholes set close together and passing into the water *side by side*. Of each group of three rowers Number One, with the largest oar, would sit slightly nearer the centre of the ship, slightly further astern, and perhaps at a slightly higher level than Number Two, and Number Two, pulling a rather shorter oar, would be similarly situated in relation to Number Three, who sat nearest to the ship's side with the shortest oar of all. Perfect rhythm would be essential or the oars would clash; but, if all went well,

---

VENETIAN 'TRIREME' (*see opposite*)

In the late Middle Ages it seems that ships were built and rowed on a system similar to that described above and in all probability derived from the Ancient Greeks. This picture is taken from a model of such a ship; and shows the triplets of rowers as viewed from above.

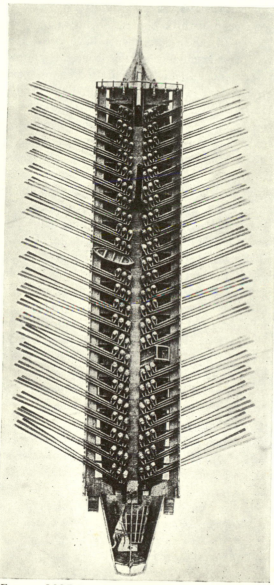

FIG. 19. MODEL OF A VENETIAN 'TRIREME'

the combined sweep of three blades, moving as one, would be extremely powerful, and experiments have proved it. The rowers were normally citizens drawn from the poorest class. In an acute crisis slaves might be drafted in on promise of earning their freedom. A coxswain shouted the orders to the rowers, aided by a piper who gave time for the oar-beat; and great precision was needed to give perfect unison in a choppy sea. Athenian crews were more highly trained than those of other states; and the tactics which in consequence they were able to develop gave them a marked superiority in war.

The old-fashioned method had been to lay the ship alongside the enemy and leave the boarding-party of marines to fight it out on the deck. But with their power of manœuvre, the more skilful Athenian crews preferred not to grapple. They used to circle round the vessel of their slower-moving enemy and ram it in the rear; or, passing alongside and suddenly shipping their own blades, crash through its oar-banks with devastating effect. Here is the description of a sea-battle in which an Athenian squadron defeated a much larger body of Peloponnesian ships.

'*The Peloponnesians arranged their ships in a circle, turning prows outwards and sterns inwards and leaving no possible inlet. The Athenians ranged their vessels in a single line and sailed round and round the enemy, driving him into a narrower and narrower space, almost touching as they passed and leading his crews to suppose that they were on the point of charging. . . . When a breeze sprang up, the Peloponnesian ships fell at once into confusion; ship dashed against ship and they kept pushing one another with long poles. There were cries of 'Keep clear!' and noisy abuse, so that nothing could be heard of the word of command or of the coxswains giving the time; and the difficulty which the inexperienced rowers had in lifting their oars in a heavy sea made the vessels disobedient to the helm. At this moment the Athenians charged and, after sinking one of the admiral's ships, had very soon made havoc of them all.*'

The skill of their shipwrights had much to do with the Athenians' success; and, as the life of a trireme was short, a large number of craftsmen must have been absorbed by this industry. The harbour of Athens, known as the Piraeus, was a splendid rock-girt roadstead, lying about five miles from the city. Here were rows of warehouses and other buildings; and even in peace-time the quay-sides must have been the scene of much bustling activity. Aristophanes, the comic poet, gives a lively description of what occurred at the outbreak of war:

> *Tramp of troops and skippers' bawl,*
> *Rations round and pay for all.*
> *Pandemonium in the sheds,*
> *Coats of gilt for figure-heads,*
> *Rowlock-pads, and casks for sale,*
> *Olives, garlic, onions, ale,*
> *Nosegays smart and pretty wenches,*
> *Fisticuffs and blackened eyes,*
> *Hammering of pegs in benches,*
> *Whistles, pipers, coxswains' cries,*
> *Noise sufficient to raise Cain,*
> *Till the dockyards rang again.*

In 415, half-way through her war with Sparta, Athens fitted out an expedition for the conquest of the island of Sicily. Thucydides' account of its departure is famous: '*When all was ready, silence was proclaimed by the sound of a trumpet, and all with one voice before setting sail offered up the customary prayers; these were recited not in each ship, but by a single herald, the whole fleet accompanying him. On deck the officers and men, mingling wine in bowls, made libations from vessels of silver and gold. The multitude of citizens and other well-wishers on land joined in the prayer. The crews raised the War-chant and when the libations were completed put out to sea; and after sailing for some distance in single file the ships raced with one another as far as Aegina.*'

The expedition failed. Not one of its members ever saw their homes again; and the disaster was the beginning of Athens' tragic downfall.

VI

DAILY LIFE IN ATHENS

I. CLIMATE, CLOTHES, HOUSES, ETC.

To appreciate the conditions of a people's daily life it is essential to know something of their climate. The climate of Attica, as of the rest of Greece, was extremely dry. For a month or two in winter there might be rains, or even snow which, though soon melted on the plains, would linger on the hill-tops. Occasionally, too, in summer, thunder-clouds would suddenly gather and come down in a deluge, sending swollen torrents racing down the ravines among the mountains. Otherwise, however, these torrent-beds are waterless, and even the rivers for the most part a mere trickle. For during spring, summer, and autumn cloudless skies last day after day. Dawn rises fresh and cool, with an invigorating sparkle in the air giving a sense as of clear spring water. But long before noon the sun is scorching hot and the whole country-side athirst. Lizards creep out of the wall-crannies to bask; crickets chirrup loudly among the grasses; and underfoot the dust lies inches deep. The afternoon wanes and then the sun goes down in a glory of molten gold. A flush steals over the hoary foliage of the olives. On the Citadel the temple of the goddess Athena catches the last rays and its marble pillars turn rosy with the glow. Behind them the huge mass of Mount Hymettus changes from blue to violet and from violet to deep purple, till darkness falls suddenly, and under a starry sky the plain resounds with the chorus of frogs croaking in the marshes.

The influence of such a climate may be traced in many aspects of the Athenians' daily life. Their clothing, in the first place,

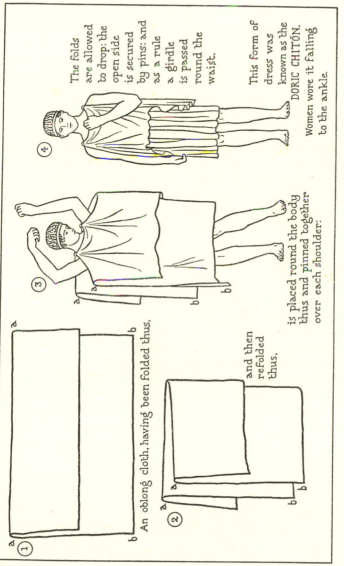

An oblong cloth, having been folded thus,

and then refolded thus.

is placed round the body thus and pinned together over each shoulder:

The folds are allowed to drop: the open side is secured by pins: and as a rule a girdle is passed round the waist.

This form of dress was known as the DORIC CHITŌN. Women wore it falling to the ankle.

FIG. 20

was admirably adapted to its alternations of heat and occasional cold. Their normal dress consisted of two garments, each of which was nothing more elaborate than an oblong piece of woollen cloth. The undergarment or tunic was doubled round the body, pinned over each shoulder, and its hanging folds caught and held in place by a girdle at the waist. The men's tunic fell to the knee, the women's lower. Workmen would disencumber their right arm by undoing one shoulder-pin and leaving the right breast and shoulder bare. Over the tunic was thrown a cloak of somewhat thicker material which in winter could be wrapped tightly round the body or in summer so arranged as to leave the limbs more free. Workers would of course dispense with the cloak while at their labour; and persons who aped the Spartan reputation for toughness sometimes did without the tunic. Sandals and boots of various types were worn; but not hats, except on a journey. For sport and exercise it was usual to strip completely. The Greeks were quite innocent of shame about the exposure of the body; and even at public games the athletes appeared naked.

In the second place, the character of the climate influenced to a large degree the planning of private houses.[1] The country-house, it is true, still followed the simple plan of the Homeric Age, and consisted of a living-room with a central hearth and a courtyard surrounded by a pent-house or veranda. In the city, where space was precious, such a lay-out was impracticable; and the Greeks, feeling the need for air and sunlight, placed the court-yard in the centre of their houses, surrounding it, as before, by a veranda supported upon stone or wooden pillars. In this miniature cloister there was shade to be found in summer and shelter from winter winds. Meals might be taken there; and much of the household business, such as spinning and so forth, done. But there was usually a large room for dinner-parties

---

[1] *Oikia* or *oikos* (= house) is found in such words as 'economy' (=oeconomy), the rules of running a household.

adjoining. The sleeping rooms opened off the central court; and the womenfolk had separate quarters on the side farthest from the front door. Light filtered into the rooms through the doorways opening on the courtyard. Externally, beyond a small spy-hole for the porter, there were no windows; and the house presented a blank wall to the street. Apart from the front door, which might be supported or flanked with pillars, there was no attempt at outside decoration; and the favourite building-material was unbaked brick, so far from durable that burglars went to work by *digging* through the walls.

At a later age, indeed, private houses grew more pretentious in style; but in the fifth century B.C. they were of an extreme simplicity. The Greeks did not choose to employ their agile wits in devising aids to physical comfort, which they affected to despise as more suitable to the soft, luxurious races of the East. There was no regular heating-apparatus, such as the Romans used; in winter-time a brazier of charcoal was carried into the rooms. Bathing was generally done at the public bath-house or the gymnasium. The rooms, as we have hinted, must have been exceedingly draughty; for only curtains seem to have covered the doorways. The floors were of beaten earth and there were no carpets. Furniture, if elegant, was austere, consisting mainly of stools, benches, and chests. There was no drainage system whatever. Slops were thrown into the street with a warning cry to passers-by; and the narrow winding alleys of which Athens was composed must have been very insanitary.

In the third place the climate favoured an open-air life, and the Athenians took full advantage of the fact. The indoor man and stay-at-home was regarded as a churl. Everywhere there was an atmosphere of genial sociability, very different from the life of our great towns and suburbs where neighbours often scarcely know one another to speak to. '*We have no sour looks for those around us,*' said Pericles in a famous speech which he made in praise of the Athenian character. As Greek cities went, the population of Athens was very large; but even so most citizens must have known a large number of their fellows by sight. As in a public school, there were characters that every one recognized—the fat man Cleonymus, or Cleisthenes the effeminate fop. Comic playwrights could always raise a laugh by alluding to them. There were nicknames, too, by which even adults were known—the Bat and the Monkey, and so forth. Men fell naturally into social sets—the young bloods, for instance, who belonged to aristocratic families, wore their hair long and rode in the cavalry. Young men formed themselves into clubs, calling themselves fancy names, such as 'the Rips' or 'the Independents', and would amuse themselves by waylaying inoffensive folk at nights. But on the whole there was very little snobbery or social exclusiveness at Athens. As Plato's dialogues show, men formed readily into groups and did not stand on ceremony with a stranger. The gymnasium and wrestling-ground were common resorts. When Socrates got back from the wars, so Plato relates, he went straight to one of these and every one jumped up to greet him and ask the news from the front. Conversation never flagged. For the Greeks were never so happy as when talking. Some of the more old-fashioned no doubt maintained a dignified gravity of demeanour; but the majority, as we may guess, were less restrained; and their excitable chatter would doubtless be accompanied, as it is to-day, by frequent shrugs of the shoulders and lively gesticulation of the hands. For they were a race of actors born. They were no mere loungers, preferring always to stand rather than sit, which they considered a slavish posture. Often, while talking, they would pace up and down, wheeling in a regular line if there were many of them. Walking was a very popular form of exercise; and they thought nothing of a tramp to the Piraeus, five miles off, and back again. Here is a delightful account which Plato gives of a stroll by the Ilissus, one of the sluggish rivers which flows hard by the city:

'*Come, friend,*' says Socrates, '*have we not reached the plane-tree towards which you were to lead us? A fair resting-place, in sooth, full of summer sounds and scents. Here is the lofty and spreading plane, and the* agnus castus *high and clustering, in fullest bloom and the greatest fragrance; and the stream which flows beneath the plane-tree is deliciously cool to the feet. Judging by the ornaments and images the spot must surely be sacred to Acheloüs and the Nymphs. How delightful is the breeze—so very sweet; and there is a sound in the air shrill and summerlike which makes answer to the chorus of the* cicadas. *But the greatest charm is the grass, like a pillow gently sloping to the head. My dear Phaedrus, you have been an admirable guide.*'

But, if the Greek could appreciate the country-side, he perhaps loved the city more; and his favourite resort was the market-place or Agora. It lay in the middle of Athens, close under the northern slope of the Acropolis itself. At that end were several important public buildings, such as the hall in which the State-Council held its sessions. Along the sides were colonnades with stately rows of pillars and brightly frescoed walls. One, the Painted Stoa, gave its name to the Stoic philosophers who originally foregathered and found their pupils there. In the central space are set rows of temporary stalls and booths. Here the country-folk bring their produce to sell. In one part will be greengrocers' stalls; in another bakers'. Fish-mongers have a pitch to themselves, with a crier to ring his bell when the market is open. Elsewhere bankers and money-changers erect their tables; and much commercial business is done. Everywhere is a babel of voices; and at time of full market the whole space is crowded. Many walk up and down in the adjacent colonnades. Groups form; and conversation flows freely, ranging over all manner of topics, from vulgar gossip to political or even philosophic discussion.

An Athenian's day began at dawn or earlier; for oil-lamps were a poor substitute for sunlight which few could afford to waste. Fast was broken by a sop of bread dipped in wine, corresponding to the coffee and roll with which the continental folk of modern times begin their day. Thus fortified, our citizen friend (whom we will suppose to be a man of means and so of ample leisure) would sally forth from his house. First, perhaps, he would pay a call on some friend; but sooner or later he would make his way to the market. He would carry a staff; and if particular about his dress, he would be at some pains to drape the folds of his cloak in the approved style of the day. He would walk, too, at a dignified pace; for a bustling gait was thought vulgar and Socrates was much ridiculed for swinging his arms in the air. A slave or two would probably be in attendance; and friends would soon fall in alongside.

Our citizen's first destination would be the barber's shop. Among Greeks shaving was not the fashion until Alexander the Great set it. But great care was lavished on the dressing of the hair; and, as a Persian spy noted with surprise on the eve of the battle of Thermopylae, even the Spartans spent much time in combing and plaiting their long tresses. Another operation performed at the barber's was treatment of the eyes for ophthalmia, a complaint rendered very common by the dust of the streets. While awaiting his turn, our friend would chat with many others who were similarly engaged. The barber's shop was a recognized centre for picking up gossip; and the news of the disaster which befell the Athenian expedition to Sicily was first learnt from a casual stranger who landed at the Piraeus and dropped into a barber's for his toilette.

By this time—about nine a.m.—the market would be filling. Purchases would be made and sent home by a slave. Business might be done at the banker's. Then, at noon, it would be time for lunch—a light meal which men often preferred to bring with them and eat in the open rather than return home again. After lunch some Greeks enjoyed a siesta; and history tells of a town which was captured by surprise attack when the inhabitants

FIG. 21. PALAESTRA SCENE

In the centre are two wrestlers, on the left a youth in the attitude of preparing to jump, on the right a javelin-thrower.

were engaged in their midday nap. But in the Athens of Pericles' time the habit was not much approved.

As the afternoon wore on, exercise was taken as a prelude to supper. Public gymnasia were available for all; and here even the middle-aged would strip for various forms of sport, of which more shall be said in a succeeding chapter. There is an entertaining vase-painting in one of our museums which depicts a man undressing while a bystander points derisively at the ridiculous proportions of his extremely rotund figure.

Exercise over, a bath followed. A slave would be in attendance with the indispensable oil-flask (for oil in those days served the purpose of soap). First he would anoint his master's body liberally, then scrape away both grease and dirt together with a metal instrument or strigil. A cold douche from a pitcher would complete the cleansing process. Warm baths, which came into fashion towards the end of the fifth century, were denounced by the more conservative as a demoralizing innovation.

II. MEALS

Dinner, which was the chief meal of the day, began in late afternoon. In sociable Athens it was usual to ask guests to share it. Men alone were invited; and no respectable lady ever took her meals in the company of male visitors. The dining-room would be arranged with couches; for the Greeks reclined at length for meals, propping themselves on the pillows so as to leave the right arm free. First, sandals would be removed, and the feet, dusty from the walk through the street, would be washed by slave attendants. Next, garlands for the head would be handed round; and then the food would be brought in on small stools or tables, one for each diner. The Greeks, unlike the Romans, were comparatively light eaters. They had a positive distaste for butcher's meat; and an army campaigning in a foreign country where no other diet was procurable felt itself hardly used. Occasionally, perhaps, at festival-time, when a sheep or pig was sacrificed, mutton or pork would follow at supper. But normally nothing more solid than sausage or black-pudding was in favour. Eggs, fish, cheese (with sometimes hare or pigeon) were the staple dishes. The working class was much addicted to broth and a sort of barley-meal porridge. Fresh fish, supplied from the local shores, could be bought in the market; but as a rule the Athenians preferred it salted and dried like bloaters. Their taste seems to have been for strong savours. Of all vegetables— and these they ate in great quantities—they preferred the garlic, a disgustingly pungent herb. Most dishes were heavily drenched with olive-oil, which also filled the place of butter for frying. Honey was used for sweetening. For special occasions more elaborate dainties were prepared, and we hear of an omelette which was compounded of milk, eggs, flour, brains, fresh cheese, and honey cooked in rich broth, and served up in a fig-leaf wrapper.

No forks or knives appeared on the diners' tables. A carver dissected any viands which required it. Fingers did the rest; but sometimes ladles moulded out of bread did duty for spoons, and after use were thrown on to the floor. When appetites were satisfied, slaves swept up all the refuse, removed the tables, and brought them in again laden with dessert. This consisted of nuts, olives, figs, cakes, and sweet-meats, but these only as an accompaniment to the drinking which followed. Greek wine, as we have said, was a rich, syrup-like fluid, and was almost invariably diluted with water. Only the semi-civilized inhabitants of Macedon in the north took their drink neat. Wines varied in quality, the best hailing from the islands of Lesbos, Chios, and Rhodes. In some brands, as in modern Greece, resin was added, giving a tart flavour. The drinking was organized according to regular rules. A 'master of the feast' was chosen by lot, and he dictated the proportion in which water and wine should be mixed—most usually in the ratio of two to one. The mixing was done by the slaves in a large earthenware bowl. From this the drink was ladled into the cups—broad shallow saucers raised on a delicate base, often of exquisite design and picked out with beautiful painted pictures.

The carouse would often last well on into the night. But the wine was, for a while at least, more apt to stimulate than to befuddle the brain; and witty talk was the rule. Sometimes, if we may judge from the dialogues of Xenophon and Plato, all manner of serious topics were discussed. In Xenophon's account of a banquet, '*when the tables were removed and the guests had poured a libation and sung a hymn, there entered a man from Syracuse to give them an evening's merriment. He had with him a fine flute-girl, a dancing-girl, and a very handsome boy who was expert at the cither and at dancing. The boy and girl first played, and all agreed that both had furnished capital amusement.*' Then, after a little talk, '*the girl began to accompany the dancer on the flute and the boy at her elbow handed her hoops which, as she danced, she kept throwing into the air, and catching again in regular rhythm. Finally a hoop was brought in, set round with upright swords, and the dancer, to the dismay of the onlookers, turned somersaults into the hoop and out again.*' '*After this admirable entertainment,*' says Socrates then, for he was one of the diners, '*should we not attempt to entertain one another?*' and invites the host to give a sample of his wit, and explain what skill or science of his own he is wont to set most store by. '*Certainly,*' replies the host, '*I will tell you my own chief pride. I believe I have the power to make men better.*' '*Make men better?*' cries another, '*By teaching them a handicraft or developing their characters, I'd like to know?*' and so the discussion begins which ranges on through a debate about Beauty and Love. At the 'Banquet' described by Plato the conversation centred round similar topics, and led to noble flights of philosophic argument.

Though exhibitions of dancing and so forth were frequently provided, it was also usual for the guests, as Socrates suggested, to furnish their own entertainment. Singing to the lyre was

Fig. 22. A BANQUET

Three men recline on slender couches. A boy-slave pours wine into the drinking-cup of one; a girl-slave plays on the pipes.

an accomplishment of which most educated Athenians were
capable. One favourite pastime was for the guests to sing round
in turn, each singer capping the last with a song more or less
connected in theme. Many of these drinking-songs were very
beautiful; and here is a sample which must suffice:

> *Fruitful earth drinks up the rain;*
> *Trees from earth drink that again;*
> *Sea drinks air, and soon the sun*
> *Drinks the sea and him the moon.*
> *Is it reason then, d'ye think,*
> *I should thirst when all else drink?*

The asking of riddles was another form of diversion. Sometimes, too, games were played. The favourite after-dinner
game was the 'Cottabos'. A little figure or mannikin was stuck
up on the end of a tall pole and the revellers tried to see which
could strike it with wine-dregs flipped out of their goblets. As
each made his throw he called a toast to some love, 'This to the
fair So-and-so.' Occasionally the wine got the better of the
drinkers and the evening ended in a sad debauch. The conclud-
ing passage of Plato's 'Banquet' gives a strange picture. '*A band
of revellers entered and spoiled the order of the banquet, compelling
every one to drink large draughts of wine. Some of the guests went
away; but Aristodemus* (who is telling the story) *fell asleep.
Towards daybreak he was awakened by the crowing of the cocks,
and found all the others had gone to sleep, save Socrates, Aristophanes, and Agathon, who were drinking out of a large goblet which
they passed round. Socrates was discoursing to them; and the chief
thing that Aristodemus could remember (for he was only half awake)
was the philosopher compelling the other two to acknowledge that
the genius of comedy and tragedy were really the same and that the
true artist would excel in both. To this they consented perforce,
being more than a little drowsy and not quite understanding the
argument. Then first Aristophanes dropped off, and finally Agathon:*

and Socrates, having laid them both on the floor, got up and went his way.'

In spite of this, the Athenians were not a gross race, even in their cups. Their exuberant spirits sometimes ran into excess; but mere drinking for drinking's sake they left to the mighty topers of the north. It was not for nothing that they wove round the personality of the wine-god Bacchus many beautiful legends of symbolic mythology: and some of their most graceful poems were concerned with the theme or the imagery of the drinking-bout. One example may here be given, which the reader will doubtless know better in its Elizabethan guise, but which will best, perhaps, be reproduced in a plain prose translation—much closer to the more restrained and more exquisite original.

'No wine-bibber I; but, if you would make me drink, taste first and pass to me and I will take it. For if you will touch it with your lips, no longer is it easy to keep sober or to escape the sweet wine-bearer; for the cup carries me the kiss from you and tells me of the favour that it had.'

VII

WOMEN AND SLAVES

FROM what has been said already it will be clear that Athenian citizens enjoyed considerable leisure; and it is natural to inquire how this came about. The explanation lay partly in the character of their occupations. Farmers, for example, were not always busy; there were slack times between corn-harvest in May and the vintage in September, and again after the vintage till the olive-picking in late autumn. Sailors, similarly, were unoccupied during winter when storms made the sea unsafe. The craftsmen, being independent and not working for a regular employer, were masters of their own time, and could knock off work when they chose. Retail dealers, too, could close their shops to attend a political meeting or dramatic performance. The Greeks knew

well enough—what modern folk are sometimes apt to forget—
that 'a pennyworth of ease is worth a penny'. Furthermore, we
must remember that the work of the home was done by the
womenfolk. In well-to-do households these were assisted by
slaves; and there was a small class of really rich men who owned
a large number of slaves and were under no necessity to work
at all. Slaves and women therefore played a highly important
part in the background of Athenian life; and it will be well to
say something here of both in turn.

I. WOMEN

The position of women at Athens in the fifth century, and,
indeed, in all Greece except Sparta, was very much lower than
in the times of which Homer wrote. The home was very strictly
their sphere; and life for them extended very little beyond it.
It was considered improper, as we have seen, for respectable
women to share the social entertainments of the men. Even if
caught in the courtyard of the house by a male visitor, they
would scuttle to the seclusion of their own apartments. They
could only walk abroad in the streets if accompanied by a slave
or other attendant. It was their business, as Pericles said in a
speech recorded by Thucydides, to be 'spoken of as little as
possible, whether for good or ill'.

During her maiden days an Athenian girl would remain
constantly under the eye of her mother and learn to fulfil her
domestic duties. She might never, like the stalwart Spartan
maidens, share the sports and amusements of the boys. Her
appearances in public would probably be confined to carrying
a basket of flowers or a pitcher of water in some religious
procession. Marriage was the inevitable goal to which her whole
life tended. To remain a spinster was the worst disgrace which
could befall a woman. When the two sexes saw so little of each
other, love matches were out of the question; and the betrothal
was arranged by the parents as a strictly business contract. The

FIG. 23. A MAIDEN

Sitting on a cushion and clad in long tunic or *chiton* and voluminous cloak,
she is engaged in burning incense over a lamp.

amount of the dowry which the bride would bring with her had an important influence upon the intending husband's choice.

The wedding itself was a cheerful ceremony. The bride's girl friends would bring her presents; and a middle-aged dame— the female counterpart to the 'best man' of our modern weddings —would superintend her toilette. Sacrifice and prayers were offered at the domestic altar; and then the bride and bridegroom sat down in the company of the family friends to a light repast of sesame-cakes. Male and female guests, be it noted, were kept in separate portions of the room. At nightfall all lined up in procession, and to the light of pine-flares accompanied the wedded pair to the bridegroom's house; and the maidens sang a parting serenade.

So the wife passed into her husband's keeping. Her property became his, and in the eyes of the law she possessed no independent status. Throughout her life she remained always under the tutelage of some male, and, if left a widow, returned into the charge of her father or brother. Henceforward her duties centred in the management of the home. She would superintend the work of the slaves, especially the female ones. She would attend to the making and mending of her husband's clothes. Spinning was an unfailing occupation and took the place of the knitting of to-day. A wad of raw wool, previously carded and cleaned, would be placed on the end of a tall stick or distaff; an end would be drawn out between the fingers and attached to an earthenware or metal 'spindle' shaped something like a top; the spindle would be set twirling as it hung and would twist the wool into thread under the guidance of nimble fingers. Weaving, too, was sometimes done at home; and much time would be spent in unfolding and refolding the numerous garments which were kept stored in the family chest.

LADY'S TOMBSTONE (*see opposite*)

This relief, from the Cerameicus or Cemetery of Ancient Athens, shows a seated lady examining her jewel-box.

Fig. 24. LADY'S TOMBSTONE

Personal adornment would not, of course, be neglected; for a prudent wife must maintain her attraction for her husband. So the jewellery casket would come out and perhaps the rouge-pot, too, when she expected his home-coming; and, if no male guests were invited, she might sit down at meal-time beside the couch on which her husband would lie reclined.

But, if an Athenian wife played no unimportant part in relieving her husband of domestic worries, she was most certainly no mere drudge.[1] Limited as her life was, there is no reason to suppose her downtrodden or unhappy. In the sculptured representations which we possess of Athenian matrons, they are shown as fine upstanding creatures, fit mothers for a race of wiry athletes. There is much, too, to show that marriages begun as a business contract developed into a bond of lifelong and heart-felt devotion. From Xenophon we have a charming description of a husband's preliminary advices to his ignorant young wife. '*When she came to me*', the man says, '*she was not yet fifteen years old and had lived under the strictest surveillance that she might see, hear, or inquire as little as possible. It was not enough, surely, that she should know how to weave a garment or weigh out the materials for her maids; though I'm bound to say she came to me very well trained in matters of cookery.*' . . . Then, after describing at length the good advice he had given to the girl, he ends his first lecture like this: '*The greatest pleasure to me will be this, that, if you prove yourself my superior, you will make me your servant and there will be no fear lest with advancing years your influence will wane; nay, the better companion you are to me and the better guardian of the house to our children, the greater will be the esteem in which you are held at home; and all will admire you, not so much for your good looks as for your good deeds in practical life.*'

There are many touching epitaphs which commemorate a

[1] Socrates' wife Xanthippe was a shrew and her husband was thoroughly afraid of her.

woman's life which had fulfilled this high ideal; and one may be given here:

'Atthis, who didst live for me and breathe thy last toward me, once the source of all my joy and now of tears, holy, much lamented, how sleepest thou the mournful sleep, thou whose head was never laid away from thy husband's breast, leaving Theios alone as one who is no more; for with thee the hope of our life went to darkness.'

II. SLAVES

Slaves were so numerous at Athens that some historians believe they outnumbered the free population. The greater part of them were drawn from barbarian countries, especially from Thrace, the coast-lands of the Black Sea, Asia Minor, and the Levant. Some were the captives of war; but most the victims of professional kidnappers. Foreign names were usual, such as the 'Thracian'—as we might say 'Sambo'—or descriptive nicknames like 'Sandy' or 'Carrots'. In a society where slavery was an accepted practice, few persons were likely to trouble their heads about the rights or the wrongs of it. But when they did, they argued, like the philosopher Aristotle, that barbarian peoples, being incapable of an independent political existence, were intended by nature to work in the service of the more civilized. On the other hand, public opinion did not favour the enslavement of Greeks by Greeks. It was something of a scandal, therefore, when in the bitterness of war a state would sell its prisoners into captivity.

It was a terrible day for the freedom-loving Greek when he suddenly found himself a helpless chattel at the mercy of a master who might, if he pleased, make his life unendurable. Punishments in those days were pretty brutal; the lash, the pillory, and even branding were common enough for thieving slaves or runaways. Even torture, as we have seen, was permitted by law when a slave's evidence was required in a trial. *'Treat him as you please,'* says a character in one of Aristophanes' plays,

'put hot bricks on him, pour acid down his nose, flay him, rack him,
string him up, give him the "Cat",' and, though allowance must
be made for comic exaggeration, the savage spirit of the words
tells a certain tale.

On the other hand, there can be little doubt that the Athenians
treated their slaves well. The law even safeguarded them to a
certain measure against excessive brutality. It was not permitted
to put a slave to death. Unprovoked assault laid the assailant
open to prosecution; it is probable that a legal limit of fifty
strokes was set to floggings. We are definitely told that slaves
at Athens were anything but cringing creatures. They would
even elbow passers-by out of their way in the street; and the
trouble was that it was unsafe to punch their heads; for in dress
and appearance they were so like the free-born citizens that it
was quite easy to make a mistake. In Aristophanes' play above
mentioned the comic slave called Xanthias is as pert and out-
spoken as Sam Weller in *Pickwick*; and he loses no opportunity
of scoring off his noodle of a master.

The fact is that the Athenians knew well enough that lenience
paid. Slaves worked better when well treated. In the home they
were frequently accepted almost as one of the family. Many
were given skilful and responsible jobs. Out of the score or so
of slaves whom a well-to-do citizen kept, there would be clerks
and copyists as well as menial workers. In the craft-shops, too,
large gangs of slaves were frequently employed alongside of
free-born labourers. They were even given wages and allowed
to accumulate savings, with the prospect that eventually they
might purchase their freedom. Generous masters sometimes
gave them their liberty as a reward for long service. When freed,
they enjoyed the same rights as resident foreigners; some rose
to a position of prosperous independence. One became a
celebrated banker.

There was one form of servile employment, however, which
stands by itself and which sheds a terrible sidelight on the

nature of Athens' social morality. We have spoken above of the silver mines which were situated at Laureum, near the Land's End of Attica. They were worked by private enterprise, and the actual work was done by gangs of slaves. Nicias the general is known to have owned a thousand. The lowest and most savage type, who were unfit for domestic service, were usually employed for the purpose. But, if not already brutalized, they must soon have become so under the horrible conditions of their life. The ore was extracted by the sinking of shafts and long, horizontal galleries which ran for miles under the hill-side. Down these the slaves were sent, nearly naked and shackled in chains. Lamps were carried, and, since those which have been found were calculated to burn for ten hours, that must almost certainly have been the length of a shift. Gangs were sent down in relays, so that digging continued night and day. No respite or hope of liberty was allowed them. Death must have been a merciful release. During the Peloponnesian War many thousands of Attic slaves are said to have deserted to the enemy; it is to be hoped that many mine-slaves were among them.

VIII

TRADES AND PROFESSIONS

AFTER all that has been said about the Athenian citizen's idle hours, it is high time that something should be added about his busy ones. For busy he was by nature; and when he worked, he worked with a zest. Aristocrats like Nicias, the owner of a thousand slaves, might be able to devote themselves exclusively to politics; but most Athenians had to work for a living. We will take their various callings one by one.

Agriculture must stand first. For, though the city's prosperity was based mainly on her industries and commerce, a large proportion of the inhabitants of Attica still lived on the soil.

The day of large landowners was over; and most of the farms were worked by small peasant proprietors. Home-grown crops supplied little more than a third of the corn needed by the swollen population of the capital, the rest coming from abroad. This was due mainly to the poor quality of the soil; for the Attic plains were fairly wide. The level ground could easily be ploughed with ox-teams; and sometimes even the lower slopes of the hill-side were terraced into tiny fields. Harvest took place early, sometime between April and June. The standing corn was cut, as in Homeric times, with a sickle; and, as then, threshing was done by oxen which moved round and round on a floor of beaten earth, trampling out the grain from the straw. Finally the chaff was winnowed away by a shovel-shaped fan, best used on a windy day. Olives were freely grown throughout Greece. In Attica they were sufficiently productive to allow some export of oil. The trees took sixteen years or more to mature, before a good harvest could be expected; so that a well-grown tree was particularly precious. The picking of the berries took place in late autumn. Pickers were often hired from the town, like hop-pickers to-day; for it was a long and tedious process. When picked, the berries were placed in a circular trough and crushed by the pressure of a circular stone wheel, after which the oil could be squeezed out by the application of a wooden lever. Vines were also grown both on the plains and on the terraced hill-side. As a rule they were trained on stakes or, more rarely, up trees. At the vintage, in September, the gathered grapes were placed in a wine-press which consisted of a sloping floor surrounded by a low wall. Here they were trodden under foot till the juice ran out and, trickling down the floor, was conveyed out by a channel. It was then stored in large jars and allowed to ferment into wine. Apart from agriculturalists proper, shepherds grazed their flocks of sheep and goats on the uplands; and charcoal-burners plied their trade at Acharnae, near the woods at the north end of the plain.

There was always, indeed, a certain antagonism between town and country. The city-dwellers regarded the farmers as country bumpkins, slow witted, conservative, and full of old-fashioned superstitions. The country-folk thought the city-dwellers fast

FIG. 25. PICKING OLIVES

and frivolous. In one of Aristophanes' plays a one-time farmer describes how he had married a fine lady of the town:

> *Rank was I with wool and grease,*
> *Fig-trays and foul-smelling lees,*
> *She of perfumes, frankincense,*
> *Saffron, kisses and expense . . .*
> *She would pet our son, and said,*
> *'When you drive your coach, my lad,*
> *Clad in purple, like a lord.'*
> *I would answer, 'Mark my word,*
> *When you drive your goat-herd rather,*
> *Clad in homespun like your father.'*

There was a further conflict of interest, of course, between seller and buyer. In another play we have a ludicrous burlesque of a market scene. A farmer—not of Attica, but a native of the adjacent town of Megara—is so hard hit by the war that he dresses up his two daughters as pigs and brings them to Athens. To convince the doubting purchaser he pinches them till they cry, 'Wee! Wee!' *'They're a fine pair of beasts,'* says the other at last, *'What will you take for them?'* *'A bundle of garlic for the one and half a peck of salt for the other.'* So the sale is made and, as usual, the farmer gets the worst of the deal. Transactions were not usually so speedy, however; for hard bargaining was the rule. Even in hiring a porter to carry a pack it was usual to higgle about the price to be paid. In another comedy the hero, who is setting forth upon a journey to the Underworld, encounters a corpse being carried out upon a bier. A bright idea strikes him. *'Carry my traps to Hades?'* he asks. The corpse sits up, looks at the traps, and says, *'Two drachmas for the job.'* *'Too much,'* replies the hero, *'Let's split the difference.'* *'Two drachmas or nothing.'* *'Take one and a half'*, says the other. *'Strike me alive, if I will,'* says the corpse (for clearly he could not wish himself *dead!*), and relapses on to his bier.

To give a proper idea of such business transactions a word should be said about money. Originally, as at Sparta, the Greeks had been content to use spits or lumps of metal; but they were a quick-witted race and early began to stamp these metal pieces with some symbol of guaranteed weight; and so was evolved the art of minting proper. Besides Athens, several states (such as Corinth) issued a currency of their own, each with its separate design; but the Athenian currency was most widely used throughout the Aegean basin. It was not until the Macedonian kings introduced them towards the end of the fourth century that *gold* coins were actually produced in Greece itself; but gold pieces called *Darics*, minted by the Persians, passed freely in Athens and elsewhere. The native coins of Athens were all of silver, procured from the mines at Laurium. They

were stamped on one side with Athena's head and on the other
with an owl, the goddess's favourite bird. Attic coins were
frequently known as 'owls'. 'Attic owls roosting in his rafters',

FIG. 26. GREEK COINS (actual size)

Two-drachma pieces: (1) of Messana (*obverse*, a mule-car; *reverse*, a hare),
(2) of Himera (*obv.* a cock; *rev.* a crab). Four-drachma pieces: (3) of Catana
(*obv.* head of Silenus; *rev.* Zeus and eagle), (4) of Athens (*obv.* head of
Athena; *rev.* an owl), (5) of Agrigentum (*obv.* two eagles on body of hare;
rev. charioteer).

said some one who wished to hint that a Spartan general
had been taking bribes. The standard coin was the *drachma*, roughly equivalent to our shilling. Two-drachma, four-
drachma, and even sometimes ten-drachma pieces were also
minted. The smaller coins, too, were of silver. They were called

'obols' and six obols went to a drachma. There were three-obol and two-obol pieces, rounder and plumper than a threepenny bit. Country-folk used to carry such small change pouched between cheek and gums; so that it became the fashion, at a dead man's funeral, to place an obol *in his mouth* to serve as fare-money for the mythical ferryman Charon, who was supposed to convey the soul across the river Styx to the Underworld. The equivalent value of ancient currencies as compared with our own is difficult to fix; for the value of metal was then much greater owing to its scarcity. Perhaps the best basis of comparison is to give the normal pay of various types of labour, though we must remember that an Athenian workman lived mainly on a vegetarian diet and was satisfied with very much fewer comforts than a British working-man. Menial labour was paid three obols, or half a drachma, a day—presumably a bare subsistence; jurors were paid at the same rate. An ordinary workman got one drachma a day. A highly skilled artisan as much as two and a half drachmae a day. The purchase of a slave cost anything from £4 to £40. A schoolmaster or music-teacher earned about £70 per annum. For such larger sums there were, of course, no equivalent coins, but the Athenians found it useful to employ special terms for convenience in reckoning. Thus 100 *drachmae* was called a *mina* or '*mna*' (£4); and sixty *minae* was called a talent (roughly £240). To get any idea of their purchasing power it would be necessary to multiply the English sums five or six times over, possibly more. A person who owned a capital of 50 talents was considered very rich. Pasion, the well-known banker, must have made over £1,000 a year; interest on loans was charged at the rate of one drachma on every mina monthly, i.e. 12 per cent. per annum. Besides loaning money on usury, much business was done in exchanging foreign coins for the native currency. The money-changers' tables were, as we have said, a prominent feature of the market-place. There, too the huckster's trade was of course a flourishing one; but as the business of a greengrocer and a fishmonger is much the same in all ages we need not pause to consider their calling. More important were the merchants who handled the overseas trade. A large number of these lived down at the Piraeus, which was itself a considerable city; and many of them were not Athenians born but resident foreigners or Metics. The Greeks, though they loved their homes, loved seeing the world also. It is true that they despised the 'barbarians', as they called all foreigners —the very word 'bar-bar-oi' being a scornful allusion to the incomprehensible gibberish that other nations talked. Even in their outlying settlements—at Marseilles, for instance, or on the coast of North Africa—where they lived cheek by jowl with less civilized folk, they were slow to intermarry with the native population or to adopt its lower standards of life; so proud were they of their national superiority.

Nevertheless they enjoyed the experience of going out among foreign peoples and the opportunity of telling fine tales when they came home again. Herodotus, the famous historian,[1] travelled far afield, visiting the coast-lands of the Black Sea, Egypt, and probably Mesopotamia. Far away south of Egypt a statue has been found on which Greek adventurers had scratched their names, like some ill-mannered modern tourist. As for the merchants, they sailed into every corner of the Mediterranean, and even penetrated beyond the Pillars of Hercules, as they called the Gibraltar Straits, to trade with the Spanish tribes and perhaps with the inhabitants of these islands. It would be tedious to give a detailed account of their markets; how they fetched corn from the Black Sea and perfumes and spices from the Levant, or how they carried pottery to the Crimea and to South Italy and Sicily. Their enterprise not merely formed the basis of Athens' prosperity; but long after, when Greece became a portion of the Roman Empire, it was her mariners who remained the principal carriers of Mediterranean trade

[1] Historian and history are derived from the Greek word *historia* (inquiry).

It must not be imagined, however, that the ancients were audacious navigators. They had no compass to assist them; and the fear of storms always kept them in harbour during winter months. The rising of the Pleiads in spring was the signal to set sail. Observation of the stars was their only guide at night; and, if possible, the Greek sailor preferred not to be caught at the mercy of the darkness. Avoiding open-sea voyages, he was accustomed to hug the coast-line or thread his way across from island to island, putting into harbour or hauling his ship ashore to bivouac for the night. Except for the accident of a sudden squall or the occasional necessity of a hard pull with the oar when an adverse wind set in, it was a peaceful and pleasant life—to sit astern at the tiller, and, while the light breeze puffed the mainsail, watch the smooth blue water ruffle under the vessel's wake and the grey shapes of the islands drift lazily by under the blazing summer sunshine. So, though the Greek sailor never pretended that he was not afraid of the sea, he thoroughly enjoyed his life. '*Give me a mattress on the poop,*' sang a Greek Masefield, '*and an awning overhead with the patter of the spray on it; a pot on the fire with a turmoil of bursting bubbles and a boy turning the meat, and a ship's plank for my table, and a game of pitch and toss, and the boatswain's whistle. That's the life I love and it fell to my lot but yesterday.*'

There was only one most uncomfortable danger—pirates. In another poem we find a soothsayer, when asked by a timid skipper whether his ship would make port safely, thus cautiously replying:

> *Let the ship be bran-new and the tackle be taut!*
> *Wait till summer for sailing! and then, sir, in short,*
> *If correctly you steer and no bold buccaneer*
> *You encounter, you'll come safe to port.*

Luckily the Athenian navy did much to suppress the nuisance. As for the risks of shipwreck, it was always possible to insure against those with the bankers at Athens. Profits on a cargo

were tolerably secure under normal conditions of trade; and
sometimes a big haul might be made, as when the first Greek
ship put in at the virgin-port of Tartessus, in western Spain,

FIG. 27. TOMBSTONE OF ATHENIAN SAILOR

He sits on the prow of his ship, his shield and helmet beside him.

and made a profit, so Herodotus assures us, of £15,000 on
the voyage—a sum which was worth in those days perhaps ten
times that amount.

Travel on land was, on the whole, less convenient and less
comfortable than by sea. The roads were poor; for the Greeks
did not, like the Romans, take steps to make a firm metalled
surface. Rains would furrow deep ruts; in the plains the dust
would lie inches deep; on the hills stones and rocks would make

the going very jolty. So, though carts and chariots were used,
they could seldom proceed at more than a walking pace; and it
was more common to travel on foot or on a mule or pack-horse.
Litters carried by slaves were not fashionable till much later
times, and the use of them was considered more suitable to the
effeminate oriental. Commercial purposes apart, the Greeks
were fond of paying visits to neighbouring cities, when warfare
did not forbid it. But their favourite pilgrimages were to the
great religious and athletic festivals, such as were held at Olympia
or Corinth. At such centres special quarters were provided
for the accommodation of visitors; but elsewhere the traveller
would have to put up at an inn. As in all ages, the discomfort of
inns was the butt of much ridicule. Comic poets speak of the
extortionate charges of inn-keepers; and there were other draw-
backs. 'Tell me,' says a would-be traveller in one of Aristophanes' plays,

> Tell me the taverns and the pastry-cooks,
> Routes, and fresh-water springs and wayside nooks,
> And lodging-houses where the bed-room rugs
> Contain—let's say—a minimum of bugs.

If we pass to what nowadays are called 'the professions', it
cannot be said that they were much in evidence at Athens.
Political posts, as we have seen, were filled by amateurs. There
were no barristers, if we except the men who wrote speeches
for parties at law. There was not even a priestly caste as among
the Israelites. Priests were usually elected for a term of years
to superintend some special ritual or act as caretaker to a temple;
but sometimes the privilege was confined to a particular family.
With the performance of his ceremonial duties a priest's responsibility ended; he had no mission to persuade other folk to live
better lives. Often he was chosen for his good looks and fine
figure. Besides priests, there were soothsayers and astrologers.
Nicias, the general, kept one in his private service. There were

professional reciters, corresponding to the minstrels of Homer's day; and there were, of course, schoolmasters—a little-respected class. Greek doctors were famous throughout the world, though it is probable that in the first instance much of their lore was derived from Egypt. Herodotus tells of one called Democedes who was a native of south Italy, but wandered from one place to another till he reached the court of the Persian king, whom he cured of a sprained ankle and the queen of an abscess. There was a good deal of superstition wrapped up with the practice of medicine. In a celebrated shrine of Asclepius, the God of Healing, patients were laid out in a corridor in expectation of the visit of the god, who was believed to appear at night in a snake's form and lick the diseased portion of their bodies. Many cures seem to have been effected; and tablets may still be seen which grateful patients set up; sometimes an ear or an eye, or whatever had caused the trouble, was represented in carving.

On the other hand, the professional doctors not merely understood the use of herbs, drugs, and ointments, but studied symptoms with some intelligence. One Hippocrates, who lived towards the end of the fifth century B.C., has some claim to be called the father of medicine on the score of his diagnoses of quinsy, epilepsy, tapeworm, and other diseases. Nevertheless, methods were crude, and satirists did not spare the doctors.

> Dr. Nostrum a visit did pay
> To the statue of Zeus. 'But', you'll say,
> 'Zeus is God, let alone
> That his statue is stone.'
> No matter—the funeral's to-day!

Anatomy could be little studied in a land where cremation of the dead was the invariable rule; and it was not till after Alexander's conquest of the East, when many Greeks settled in Egypt, that dissection of corpses was extensively practised. Nevertheless, operations were performed, and even the wandering Democedes possessed implements. Without anaesthetics surgery must have been a grim business; and of it, too, the wits were critical:

> *The patient dead, the surgeon wiped his knife.*
> *'Poor chap,' he said, 'he'd have been maimed for life.'*

We next pass on to the handicrafts[1]—the true pride and glory of Athens. And first, we must disabuse our minds of any modern conceptions of industrial relations. There were not at Athens a class of employers and a class of employed. A free-born worker was too jealous of his independence to accept the position which Socialists of to-day would call 'wage-slavery'. He would hire out his services when and where he chose—to the state it might be or to some private contractor—but remained his own master. In the workshop, it is true, apprentices and assistants would gather round a master-craftsman to learn and practise the trade till they were fit to set up on their own. Men of the same craft, too, joined in associations or guilds, cherishing the secrets of its technique, holding common religious rites, and dwelling, as a rule, in some separate quarter of the town. The metal-workers, for instance, would live near the temple of Hephaestus, god of smiths. The potters' quarters, known as the Cerameicus, can still be identified. No industry at Athens was more flourishing, and a word must be said on the subject.

Near the city, as luck so fell, there were extensive beds of fine potter's clay. Modelling was done on a wheel, and it is impossible to exaggerate the beauty of the vessels produced. They were of all shapes and sizes, and for the most part intended for everyday use, such as drinking-cups, mixing-bowls, oil-jars, and so forth. But they were of exquisite design; and there are

---

[1] A craft or art was called *technē*, whence our own words 'technical' and 'technique'.

TYPICAL VASES (*see opposite*)

(1) Panathenaic amphora for holding oil, (2) Kylix or drinking-cup, (3) Krater, for mixing wine with water.

FIG. 28. TYPICAL VASES

no more priceless treasures in our modern museums than the Attic, Corinthian, or other Greek vases. When the potter had finished with the vase, it was handed to the painter to adorn. The actual surface of the clay was a pale red or ochre, and on this the painter picked out his design in a rich black lustre. In early days it had been the custom to paint the patterns and even the human figures in black silhouette; but presently it had been perceived that the latter at any rate would look far more lifelike if the black were used for the background and the figures left in the flesh-coloured tint of the natural clay-surface. All manner of scenes were depicted; some drawn from mythology, some from every-day life. But such was the imaginative genius of the artists that no two were ever alike. There was no idea of cheap mass-production at Athens. Every vase was a work of art in itself. Some of the artists appended their signatures. But, though their names are now famous, they were of little account in those days. The reward of the humble craftsman was simply the artist's satisfaction in work superbly done.

Next, the builders. In these early days religious architecture took precedence of all other forms. True, under Pericles a great Entrance Gate was built on the Acropolis; but even this was merely a further adornment of the sacred precinct; and the principal achievements of the age were the temples which were erected there.

The normal plan of a Greek temple was severely simple—a plain rectangular shrine, the roof of which projected several feet outwards and was carried on all four sides[1] by a continuous row

---

[1] Sometimes only on two, and with columns therefore only at the two ends.

DORIC ARCHITECTURE (*see opposite*)

A corner of the Parthenon. Note the fluted columns without a base: the bowl-shaped 'capital' supporting the superstructure or 'entablature': the series of 'triglyphs' or grooved slabs alternating with square bas-reliefs called 'Metopes', now much damaged: above these, the spring of the gable or 'pediment', originally containing a group of statues, of which only fragments are still *in situ*.

Fig. 29. DORIC ARCHITECTURE

of columns. The columns were 'fluted' with grooves which, catching the light, give a pleasing sense of variety; and on the top of each, supporting the masonry which held the roof, was a 'capital' of various design. The three different types of capital mark the three different styles of architecture. In the Doric style—plain, massive, and dignified—the capital was no more than a shallow basin-shaped cushion. In the more delicate Ionic style, it curled out on either side in 'volutes', not unlike a pair of ram's horns. In the Corinthian—a later style, very rich and ornate—the capital was carved to represent a bunch of acanthus leaves. The Doric style was most favoured by Athenian architects of the fifth century; and in this style was built the great temple of the goddess Athene which stood on the Acropolis and which was known as the Parthenon. The Parthenon is still standing; and even in its present state of decay it is a building of extraordinary grandeur—a sight which no one who has once seen it can ever forget. To attempt to describe its beauty in words is impossible; but one or two things may be noted which contributed thereto.

In the first place, the Athenian builders were fortunate in possessing—no farther off than the slopes of Mount Pentelicus at the head of the Attic plain—quarries of exquisite creamy-white marble. The masonry and pillars of the Parthenon, which were made of this material, have long since weathered to a beautiful golden tinge; but in the days when they were first set up their sparkling purity, standing clear-cut against the deep blue sky, must have been infinitely more impressive. Painted patterns, too, adorned the surfaces in a manner which the ancients found pleasing, though the modern eye may prefer the marble unstained.

In the second place, though massive and simple in design, the Parthenon was of rare workmanship. The apparently straight lines of which it is composed are all found on closer inspection to display a subtle curve, intended to avoid tiring the eye with

FIG. 30. IONIC ARCHITECTURE

The north-west porch of the Erechtheum. Note the slender grooved
columns on a base: the capital with double 'volutes' much damaged: the
light 'entablature', along which once ran a frieze of figures set against a
background of black marble.

flat monotony and to correct the optical effect of sagging which a straight line is apt to give. No mortar was used; and the drums of which the columns are composed are fitted so tightly together that even a needle can scarcely be thrust into the crack. The fluting of the columns, too, and every other detail have been chiselled with a delicate precision which no modern mechanical methods could rival.

Lastly, the Parthenon was adorned with sculptured figures, themselves masterpieces of artistry. In either gable-end were set large groups of statues representing gods and goddesses. At intervals along the masonry which supported the roof were other smaller groups;[1] and beneath the colonnade, high on the outer wall of the shrine itself, ran a continuous frieze of figures in bas-relief. Many of these sculptures were removed from the ruins of the temple during the early part of the last century; and they may now be seen in the British Museum. The designer and general controller of these works was a sculptor called Pheidias; but how far he actually carved them with his own hand is uncertain. We can distinguish among them the hands of many assistants; for, like the potters and other artisans, the sculptors, too, seem to have worked in the studio of a master-craftsman, learning and imitating his methods. It was one of the chief reasons for the Greeks' artistic excellence that each individual artist did not attempt to strike out a wholly new line of his own, but was content to follow in a set tradition, reproducing the same type of statue as his master, but adding here and there some small improvement of his own. In this way a steady progress was maintained towards complete mastery of technique.

The decoration of buildings was only one department of the sculptor's art. Individual statues of gods or human beings were also set up in sacred precincts or in public squares. Some were

[1] These smaller groups are known as 'metopes', the gable-ends as 'pediments'.

FIG. 31. A GREEK YOUTH

of marble, some of bronze. Pheidias himself was commissioned to execute a colossal bronze statue of Athene, which stood near the entrance of the Acropolis. His most famous masterpiece, however, was another gigantic figure of the goddess which was placed in the interior of the Parthenon and which was made of much more valuable materials. It was of gold and ivory, gold for the draperies and ivory for the flesh, thin layers of either substance being fixed upon a core of wood. This colossus has, of course, long since disappeared; and, indeed, there are very few[1] statues by the more celebrated masters still surviving. But even from the copies which later sculptors made of them, as well as from the works of less celebrated artists, we can realize something of what the Greeks' genius was. They were greatly assisted, no doubt, by the fact that in the gymnasium and elsewhere they could study the anatomy and movements of human bodies—and human bodies trained to an extraordinary degree of muscular perfection. But they were by no means content with mere lifelike imitation. They strove to produce an ideal type, more beautiful than any individual human body. The artist Polycleitus, for instance, fashioned a statue of a naked athlete which was considered in antiquity to embody the perfect proportions of the male figure. Nor was physical perfection alone considered. Pheidias himself erected at Olympia a colossal statue of Zeus, so dignified and majestic that men said that merely to have seen it was a religious education. It must not be thought, however, that artists alone were conscious of such qualities. In the production of great art an appreciative

---

[1] The Hermes of Praxiteles is one instance of a statue by a well-known master.

ACROPOLIS FROM NORTH-EAST (*see opposite*)

The modern town lies on the site of ancient Athens; the Agora would be situated on the right side of the picture. On the Acropolis are seen (from left to right) the Parthenon, the Erechtheum, the Propylaea or entrance gates. One of the neighbouring hills, capped by a monument, emerges beyond the Parthenon.

FIG. 32. ACROPOLIS FROM NORTH-EAST

public is needed: the Athenian people were extremely proud of the Parthenon, and Pericles was able to say of them, with unquestionable truth, that they were 'lovers of beauty'.

If by some magic we could make our way into the streets of ancient Athens, we should be chiefly struck, I fancy, by the extraordinary combination of beauty and of squalor side by side. We should observe with disgust how garbage and filth of every sort was allowed to litter the narrow roadways. Our noses would inform us of the complete absence of any drainage system. The exterior of the houses would strike us as mean; for walls of crumbling mud are not impressive. We should note the grimy limbs and faces of little children playing naked in the dust; and we should probably not be impressed by the cleanliness of the average citizen's clothes. Many of the folk would seem singularly unlike the handsome, fine-limbed creatures which our study of modern museum-cases might have led us to expect. There would even be repulsive types of humanity—beggars, cripples, men with limbs disfigured in war or with diseases hideously untended.

And then the contrast. Emerging above the low level of the surrounding houses are the stately columns and carved or painted mouldings of many a public hall or temple. Round the market-place rise the long and spacious porticoes, their walls gay with frescoed scenes. Lining the open spaces would be statues innumerable, of gods and goddesses, athletes and national heroes, of exquisite craftsmanship and beauty of design. In the market-square or through the doors of private houses we should catch glimpses of pots and jars embellished with all the richness of the craftsman-painter's fancy. Outside the city gates and lining the roadway are tombs, some bearing marble figures or scenes carved in bas-relief; others, commemorating the dead of a poorer class, with no more than a simple jar, yet as exquisite in shape as it is simple. Finally, towering above the roofs and buildings of the town itself, stands the majestic rock of the

Acropolis, and on it, serene and dazzling in the pure, smokeless air, the marble columns and gabled roofs of Portico and Temples, a miracle of loveliness, perfect alike in finish and proportion, rich with coloured patterns of crimson and blue and purple, and here and there a gilded ornament which catches the sunlight and flashes its rays far out across the plain to the surrounding mountains or over the dancing waves of the sea. Athenian mariners, voyaging homewards from distant parts and rounding the jutting rocks of the last promontory, must have felt their hearts leap as they recognized this token that they were once again nearing their incomparable town.

IX

RECREATION

I. ATHLETICS[1]

An existence which was all work and no play had no attraction for the Greek. He would have intensely disliked the drudgery of an office-stool and the mechanical monotony of modern industrial life. So, even if cessation from work meant less money in his pocket, he was jealous of his pastimes; and he had many. For the elderly and less active there were draughts, dicing, and cock-fighting. The rich kept horses and raced them, chiefly in harness. The boys had a variety of games. There was a sort of Blind Man's Buff, which went by the name of the 'Bronze Fly'. Another resembled Prisoners' Base, being played between two teams, one of pursuers, one of pursued. In literature, too, there are allusions to hoops. Toy carts are to be seen on children's tombstones; and in one passage of Aristophanes we hear of mud-houses and frogs carved out of pomegranate rind. Ball games were common; one represented on a bas-relief seems to have closely resembled hockey. Others were concerned with

---

[1] Athletics is derived from the Greek word *athlon* (='a prize given in a contest' or 'the contest' itself).

ball-throwing in various forms. The ball, too, was commonly used in dancing; and dancing was a very favourite form of exercise, much more akin to musical drill than to anything else. Though older men danced (the poet Sophocles was an adept), the chief value of such drill was for the young, and it was controlled by an instructor or trainer. The importance of learning rhythmical movement was much emphasized by Greek authors who studied educational methods. They believed that the development of character was greatly influenced by the type of tunes which were employed. Plato, in sketching the institutions of an ideal city-state, lays great stress on this; and it is clear that modern rag-time and jazz would have been completely banned.

Perhaps the most important purpose of musical drill, however, was that it inculcated the spirit of team-work and a sense of disciplined harmony with others, so essential to the good citizenship of a Greek community. It was for this reason that dancing was so much practised at Sparta.

The Competitive Spirit, on the other hand, was by no means neglected; and various forms of athletic sport gave ample opportunity for individual prowess. At Athens there were several small training-grounds for boys, called 'Palaestrae', or wrestling-schools. Outside the city, too, there were two much larger Gymnasiums—a word which simply implied a place where one might exercise 'naked'. These corresponded to our own extensive playing-fields, and were open to both men and boys. They would be surrounded by avenues of trees and colonnades containing dressing-rooms and bath-houses. On entering, the first thing was to strip and rub the body liberally with oil. Provision was made for those who merely wanted to keep fit. There would be punch-balls, for instance, consisting of a pigskin filled with sand. Those who desired a contest of skill had a wide choice. Running was, of course, a favourite exercise. The course was usually of soft sand; a test of endurance being the primary object, not a breaking of records. There were

Fig. 33. WARRIORS PLAYING DRAUGHTS

sprints and long-distance races, and, as a training for the hoplite-soldier, a race in full armour. The long jump was practised, but never the high jump. The jumper apparently took no run, but held in his hands two weights of stone or metal which he could throw behind him when in mid-air and thus give his body an extra impetus. Again, there were javelin-throwing and quoit-throwing. The javelin was wound round with a leather thong, which, being held firm by a finger at the moment of discharge, imparted a rotatory motion, giving greater length and perhaps greater accuracy. Distance alone mattered in throwing the quoit. It was a circular disk of stone or metal, which was swung with a single step forward and with the exertion of every muscle in the body. Boxing was popular except at Sparta. In friendly bouts, it is true, a cap was worn for the protection of the ears; and round the hands were wound long strips of leather, but these merely to save the knuckles, not to soften the blow. Sparring after the modern fashion was unknown; the hands were held high above the head and brought down right and left on the opponent's guard. Wrestling was equally popular; and most of the throws familiar to modern wrestlers were employed—the Flying Mare, the Heave, and the Cross-buttock. Here is the description of an ancient wrestling match: '*When the Ethiopian came at him again, he made as though to fall flat on his face; . . . and then when he lifted his arm to take hold of him, putting his right arm under his left side, the other by lifting up his hand overthrew him in a heap and casting himself under his arm-pits gripped him and with his heels forced him to fall upon his knees; then leaping on his back and clasping his feet about his stomach made him stretch out his legs to stay himself, and finally pulling his arms over his head behind him laid him flat on his belly on the earth.*'

Most interesting of all, however, was the combination of boxing and wrestling known as the Pancration. In this very brutal form of sport any means of vanquishing an opponent

FIG. 34. ANCIENT 'HOCKEY'

were permitted, except biting or gouging out his eyes. So fierce was the struggle that sometimes men were killed; and the story is told of one pancratist who allowed himself to be strangled rather than lift the finger which gave admission of defeat.

There were many opportunities even at Athens for the public display of individual prowess; for competitions and races not infrequently formed a part of religious festivals. But among all Greek athletic contests the most famous by far was that held at Olympia once in every four years. The precinct of Olympian Zeus, at which these games were held, lay some miles inland on the west coast of the Peloponnese; and there in the heat of summer a vast concourse of competitors and spectators gathered from every part of the Greek world. Booths were erected for their accommodation. Beggars, hucksters, mountebanks, and fortune-tellers all flocked in as at Epsom on a Derby Day. Even historians and professors took the opportunity to exhibit their wisdom in public. The Festival was of great antiquity, originating, it may be, in some primitive rite of human sacrifice in which, as time wore on and humaner notions grew, the victims had been permitted to fight one another instead of losing their lives. In any case, religion played no small part in the games while they were in progress, and even warring states were accustomed to suspend hostilities. They began on the first day with sacrifice at the altar of Olympian Zeus. The second day was given up to Junior Events. On the third the men's contests began—running, pancration, and others. On the fourth was held the Pentathlon, a combined test in five events—quoits, sprint, wrestling, long jump, and javelin throwing. The winner of most events was victor.

The games concluded with chariot-races for teams or single horses. The foot-races and other events were held in a stadium;

OLYMPIA (*see opposite*)

Between the wooded Hill of Cronos (on left) and the broad bed of the River Alpheus lie the ruins of the sacred Precinct among low trees. The stadium was on the farther side of these; the Hippodrome nearer the river.

Fig. 35. OLYMPIA

the horse-races in the Hippodrome hard by. On the last day the victors were proclaimed by a herald and crowned with a wreath of wild olive by the stewards of the games. That was the only official prize; but a victory at Olympia evoked boundless enthusiasm among the fellow townsfolk of the successful athlete. He was received home with the most extravagant rejoicings. He was fêted, loaded with rewards, and often provided, if he needed them, with free meals in the town-hall for life. In this matter, indeed, the Greeks were apt to abandon their habitual self-restraint; and to such a pitch did the hero-worship run that it ended by ruining the spirit of the games. Specialization set in; and the professional athlete supplanted the all-round amateur. One poet declared that the country was ruined by this new breed of 'pot-hunter'. He was apt to be a swaggering, pugnacious bully. His muscular over-development erred against the strict canons of physical proportions. He trained on a diet of meat. But the hero-worship of athletes had one admirable result. Their victories in the games were celebrated in a way which was natural to an artistic people. Artists moulded statues to be set up in commemoration of their prowess. Poets wrote odes in their honour. Here is the beginning of an ode written by Pindar on the winner of the Boys' Pancration at the Isthmian Games held near Corinth.

> *Cleander in his April prime to free*
> *From toil's effect with ransom of renown*
> *And pay the pains that won his Isthmian crown*
> *As erst his Nemean, let one of ye,*
> *Young men, awake for him the chant of victory,*
> *Soon as your revel choir are come*
> *To the pranked portals of his home.*

STADIUM AT DELPHI (*see opposite*)

The Stadium lies half in the shadow of the precipitous cliffs of Mount Parnassus. Across the nearer end of the course stretches a stone sill used for starting-point or goal in the races.

Fig. 36. STADIUM AT DELPHI

II. DRAMATIC ENTERTAINMENTS

Festal celebrations, whether accompanied by athletic contests or otherwise, were a very common feature of Athenian life. For whole days together, many times in the year, the entire city would keep holiday (and in justice to them it is only fair to remember that there were no Sundays). There were some celebrations to which women only were admitted; others in which the whole citizen-body took part. The most splendid of all was the Panathenaea, a festival held in honour of the patron-goddess Athene. Its principal event was a procession to the Acropolis, the scene of which is depicted on the great Parthenon frieze now in the British Museum. At the head of the procession went a monster ship on wheels carrying a sacred robe woven for the image of the goddess and destined to be laid, as an annual offering, upon her knees. After the ship came girls carrying baskets of scent and wine-jars, then bulls for the sacrifice, then a deputation of resident foreigners in scarlet cloaks, boys bearing pitchers, old men with olive-branches, finally a group of chariots, and, bringing up the rear, a cavalcade of youths mounted on mettlesome steeds. It is clear that the Athenian people well understood the art of organizing a spectacle of this sort.

More interesting to ourselves, however, was the Festival of Dionysus the Vine-god, at which dramatic competitions were held; and of this some fuller description must be given. The great Dionysia, as this festival was called, was not the only dramatic festival at Athens. It was held in March, and there was another which took place somewhat earlier in the year, while similar performances on a more modest scale were popular in the Attic countryside. The origin of the drama may, indeed, be traced to some simple form of rustic entertainment at which a chorus of men danced in a ring, reciting or chanting the story of some mythological episode. As time went on, a man, dressed up in appropriate robes and mounted on a table, had been

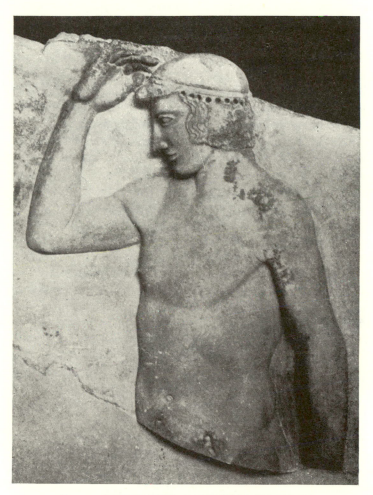

FIG. 37. BOY VICTOR CROWNING HIMSELF

introduced to impersonate this or that character in the story and to hold a crude dialogue with the leader of the chorus. He was called the 'Hypocrites'[1] or 'Answerer'; and so the history of drama proper began.

To enable him to impersonate more than one character, moreover, arrangements were made for this 'Answerer' or actor to retire into a tent behind his stage or table, and reappear in a new guise. By ancient custom both he and the chorus wore masks; and a swift transformation therefore presented no great difficulty. All the features of this primitive drama were present in the fully developed tragedy of Periclean Athens. The auditorium of the theatre, which was scooped out of the southern slope of the Acropolis, was arranged round a circular dancing-ring or 'orchestra', in which a chorus performed its evolutions. Beyond it rose a shallow stage and behind the stage a building which corresponded to the actor's tent and served as a Green Room. On it was hung or painted rude scenery, representing as a rule a palace-front—or sometimes maybe a temple—with doors opening on the stage. In the course of a play there was scarcely ever a change of scene, all the action being supposed to take place in one locality. Sometimes, however, a painted screen at either end of the palace was swung round and, by presenting a fresh picture to the audience, suggested that a new setting had been given to the stage. There were other rude devices of a mechanical sort—a lift by which gods and goddesses could be lowered as though from the sky, and, more curious still, a platform which could be pushed forward on rollers from the interior of the palace and so bring in view a tableau of some murdered person or persons; for it was a rule that no violent death might be enacted on the stage.

As this queer device has already warned the reader, the Greeks did not aim in their dramatic productions at a *realistic* representation of life; that is, they did not wish the onlooker to feel

---

[1] Hence our word 'hypocrite' (a man who 'plays a part').

FIG. 38. RIDERS IN PANATHENAIC PROCESSION (FROM PARTHENON FRIEZE)

that a *real* murder, or whatever it might be, was being enacted before his eyes; and in nothing was this more evident than in the get-up of the actors themselves. Two, or sometimes three, actors were the outside limit allowed to a playwright; so that he naturally availed himself of the opportunity of using them for a variety of characters by a quick change behind the scenes. To facilitate this a mask was still worn; and its lofty head-dress gave an imposing addition to the actor's stature. To increase this yet further, he wore on his feet a pair of club-soled boots several inches in height, but partially covered by his sweeping robes. With such encumbrances rapid movement was clearly impossible; and we must not expect to find in the Attic theatre anything resembling our own notions of a play.

If we are to suggest a modern parallel, the evolutions of the chorus may perhaps be likened to some stately movement of a Russian ballet. The actor's part, on the other hand, must have been spoken in a musical intonation with slow rhythmical gestures of the body and arms. On the elocution of the words the main effect of the play must certainly have depended, and the actor's art needed highly professional training. The play itself consisted of a series of long set speeches, varied by occasional interchange of rapid dialogue and, of course, by interludes of chorus songs. It was the poetry and passion of the words, accompanied by appropriate and carefully calculated movement, that constituted the appeal of Greek tragedy. For in an open-air theatre, with no opportunity for limelight or other scenic effects, and with actors whose masks debarred all use of facial expression, it is clear that most of the other elements which go to make a modern drama were ruled out. In this it may be that the Greeks' instinct was right. For, when we come to think of it,

---

THEATRE AT EPIDAURUS (*see opposite*)

In the foreground are the remains of the stage-buildings; beyond which lies the circular *orchestra* or dancing-ring with central altar, surrounded on three sides by the stone seats of the auditorium.

Fig. 39. THEATRE AT EPIDAURUS

the emotions are the real pith of a tragedy, and emotions are best stirred by words.[1] In a murder-scene, for instance, the real essence of the horror lies not in the blow of the knife, and the sight of the flowing blood, but in the passions of hatred and anger and the agony of desperate fear. Such things were never better depicted than by the great authors of the Attic stage. They wrote in a tone of high solemnity, befitting the great themes of which they told. It must never be forgotten that their plays were enacted at a religious festival. Their themes were drawn from mythological legends which to them were much what the Bible is to us. Even to-day, when the plays are revived and acted before a modern audience, it may be noticed that the lines are almost invariably spoken with an intonation which we usually associate with the interior of a church.

So it was for what we should call a distinctly 'high-brow' entertainment that the Athenian people gathered at the Great Dionysia; and though it was a cheerful enough occasion, and all would be in holiday mood, the demands on their attention were considerable. Proceedings began early and lasted till well past noon; and this not on one but on three successive days. For three poets or playwrights had been previously selected for the competition and on each of the three days one of them would produce not a single tragedy, but three separate tragedies, more or less loosely connected in plot. At the end of these was usually appended a fourth play (called a Satyric drama) in a somewhat lighter vein. Finally, each day's programme closed with a comedy proper.

Besides writing the plays the poet would take a hand in their production. The state provided the actors; and the cost of the training of chorus and providing clothes and so forth was assigned to some rich citizen. If public-spirited, he would take, as we have said, a considerable pride in his duties. Embroidered

---

[1] As every one knows, the best ghost-stories are those in which the mystery is suggested, but never actually described or given bodily form.

FIG. 40. TRAGIC ACTOR

Note the mask topped by a head-dress to increase the actor's height, and the club-soled boots (*kothurnoi*) serving the same purpose.

dresses, soldiers equipped in gleaming armour, suites of attendants bearing handsome painted vases, such things would
add a pleasant touch of pageantry; and it would therefore be
a spectacle of some magnificence to which the spectators might
look forward.

From early dawn the great semicircle of seats would begin to
fill up. The fee charged for admission was trifling; and most
of the city-residents, at any rate, would be there. Visitors often
came from a distance. The seats consisted of steps either carved
from the rock or constructed of wood or stone; and the use of
cushions was advisable. The space allowed per man, if we may
judge by marks still visible on the slabs, was extremely narrow;
the audience must have been packed like sardines. In the front
row, next the dancing-ring, were carved marble chairs for priests
and other dignitaries. Beyond the stage buildings (there was,
of course, no curtain) the eye might travel across some four
miles of plain to the coast and the wide horizon of the sea.

It would be past noon before the performance was over.
Then the audience would disperse, to muster again on the two
following days for a hearing of the other competitors. At the
close of the festival the verdict was given by judges specially
chosen from the whole citizen body; and it is a tribute to their
perspicacity that they very consistently assigned the prize to
the two great tragedians Aeschylus and Sophocles. Euripides,
their younger rival, was more advanced in his views and corre-
spondingly less popular. What seems certain, moreover, is that
the judges' verdict must have reflected the public taste. The
Athenians were a lively, obstreperous audience and expressed
their approval or disapproval vigorously. We even hear of one
actor who was pelted off the stage. They were critical, too, of the
least error of speech. One unfortunate actor who was guilty of a
mispronunciation no more serious than if 'when' were spoken as
'wen', was a familiar butt for ridicule. There is no more telling
indication of the high level of the Athenians' taste than their

ability to recognize quotations. For Aristophanes is constantly poking fun at Euripides by introducing tags drawn from his plays; and there can be no doubt whatever that he carried the audience with him. It is improbable that a keener or more appreciative set of theatre-goers ever existed in the history of the world.

NOTE.—In literature and art many of our modern terms are derived from the Greek. 'Drama' (from *drao* = I do) is 'a thing done or acted'. 'Tragedy' and 'comedy' are Greek words: so is 'orchestra', though it has changed its meaning. 'Poetry' comes from *poieo*, to make or invent. 'Lyric' from *lyra*, a harp to which songs were sung. Metre comes from *mĕtron* = a measure; and so on.

X

RELIGION

WE have already said something in an earlier chapter concerning the gods and goddesses of the Greeks; and this is not the place for any full description of their several characteristics and attributes. Suffice it to say that round their personalities were woven innumerable tales of wonderful beauty and rare imagination. The Greeks were great story-tellers; and throughout succeeding ages the art and literature of the world have been continually inspired by their creative genius. Roman poets drew almost entirely for their subjects on the old Greek legends. Our own Elizabethan writers are constantly alluding to the same old tales. Painters, too, have depicted them; and all know Botticelli's picture of the Birth of the Love Goddess from the Sea.

But, however imaginative, the tales which the Greeks told of their gods were not very edifying. In Homer gods and goddesses alike are represented as cheating and lying in a manner to which the human characters of the poem would seldom stoop. Zeus himself, the King of the Immortals, was perpetually engaged in discreditable love-affairs with mortal women. Half the heroes of legend were the offspring of such illicit amours; and when we further consider the character of Bacchus the Wine-god or Zeus's jealous consort Hera, we are forced to the conclusion that the influence of such a creed can scarcely have been for good. In other words, the example set by the Immortals was not such as to encourage men or women to lead better lives. The most that can be said is that folk refrained from offending the gods for fear of the consequences. It was not until philosophers like Socrates began to call in question the truth of the old legends and to substitute the idea of one supreme deity for the belief in many gods that any higher conception of divine nature became possible.

For ordinary folk, therefore, the main motive of religion was to enlist the aid or placate the anger of the Unseen Powers. The Greeks, as St. Paul observed at a much later date, were extremely superstitious. They believed profoundly in the significance of dreams. They were much addicted to the use of charms; and on his death-bed his attendants are said to have hung an amulet round the neck of the great Pericles himself. If any misfortune befell them, their first consideration was to ask which god they had offended. '*What ill omen did I encounter as I left my house this morning?*' cries a character in one of Aristophanes' plays who finds himself in trouble. Even public proceedings, as we have seen, were much affected by superstitious fancies; and the most important issues were often decided upon no better grounds. Once, when the great Athenian fleet was ready to set sail for Sicily, it was discovered that during the night unknown persons had defaced certain sacred images which

---

VIEW FROM DELPHI (*see opposite*)

The eye travels down the gorge to the narrow plain, at the left-hand extremity of which an inlet of the Corinthian gulf is just visible.

FIG. 41. VIEW FROM DELPHI

lined the streets; and the expedition was very nearly cancelled. Again, when the same expedition stood in imminent danger of defeat and the decision was made to escape by sea before it was too late, an eclipse of the moon occurred, and on the advice of the soothsayers the general Nicias refused to give the order to sail—with fatal results.

Perhaps the most interesting of all Greek superstitions was the belief in oracles. The best known of these was the oracle of Apollo at Delphi, where the ruins of the god's sacred precinct may still be seen nestling on its hill-side among wild mountain scenery, with exquisite views of the olive-clad valley beneath. Hither in ancient times came a stream of visitors to ask the god's advice on various problems. Within the temple there is said to have been a chasm through which sulphurous fumes issued. Over the chasm was placed a three-legged stool or tripod; and a priestess, seated on the stool, underwent some sort of ecstatic frenzy in which she gave inspired utterance to the god's views. The priests apparently turned her utterance into hexameter verse and then delivered it to the inquirer. There seems little doubt that the priests themselves were well posted with information about current events, gleaning it, as we may guess, through secret agents. At any rate, they were able to give extraordinarily shrewd answers and sometimes to predict coming events. Not infrequently they 'hedged' and gave an ambiguous answer which could be interpreted in two ways. The most famous instance was of a Lydian monarch who was told that, if he crossed a certain river, he would destroy a great empire. He crossed it full of confidence that he would destroy his enemy's empire; but, unluckily for himself, destroyed his own.

The answers given were sometimes surprisingly irrelevant. There was a man who was afflicted with a stammer and came to ask about a cure. He was told to go and found a colony in Libya. The parents of a lad were once assured that he would win great victories, and on the score of this advice thought of training him as an athlete; but the victories he actually achieved were won with his pen.

Religion in Greece was not, of course, confined to special occasions of crisis or perplexity. In one way or another it entered into nearly every department of daily life. Thus, no Greek would ever drink a cup of wine without first pouring out a few drops on the floor as a libation to some god. Particular deities were frequently invoked in accordance with the belief in their special powers and properties. If a man dug up a coin in his garden, he would offer thanks to Hermes, the god of treasure-trove. If he set forth on a voyage, he would put up a prayer to Poseidon, the god of the Ocean. Each craft-guild, as we have seen, had its patron-deity and would offer common worship and sacrifice at fixed times. Women, too, held ritual celebrations to which no male was admitted. Many of the national festivals were of an agricultural origin, and were intended to secure divine favour for crops or vintage. The peasantry, as we have said, were especially superstitious. They would observe certain days as propitious for sowing or other operations; and every month at the new moon would anoint themselves with oil. There was one festival, called the Apaturia, which was specially concerned with the ties of blood-relationship. On this occasion families and clans forgathered. Newly born children were presented as it were for christening; and feasts were held at which sausages were consumed in enormous quantities. Pigs were very commonly used as victims, as being best suited to the poor man's purse; but in state ceremonies, such as the Panathenaea, oxen were also sacrificed.

Tradition is slow to die. Even to-day the Greek peasant, when he takes his wine, seldom fails first to pour a few drops into the glass and tip them out ceremoniously upon the floor. He is probably quite unaware of the significance of his act; but the pagan origin of the custom cannot stand in any doubt. Nevertheless, though pagan customs may linger, paganism and

Christianity are a whole world apart. This is no place to analyse
the difference; but one striking point of contrast may at least
be noted. To the ancient Greeks the deity was something to be
regarded with awe, but not with love. At times he was not
even treated with respect. There is an extraordinary comedy
of Aristophanes, called the *Frogs*, in which the god Dionysus
himself is represented as a vulgar, drunken buffoon whose
ineptitude and cowardice form the chief humour of the play.
Needless to say, the Greeks' taste was not always as outrageous
as that. But they would never have understood the feelings of
the Hebrew who beat his breast with contrition and humbled
himself abjectly before Jehovah's presence. When they prayed
they stood erect, raising both hands skywards and speaking in a
loud, clear voice.[1] They disliked the oriental custom of grovelling
to the deity. A dignified spirit of self-reliance lurked behind this
attitude. '*Man*', said one of their philosophers, '*is the measure
of all things.*' Human life was to them a magnificent, even if a
tragic, adventure; and they had little real thought of any spiritual
life beyond. Death was an unmitigated evil, to be met, indeed,
with calm courage, but without hope of future happiness. They
believed, it is true, in an existence beyond the grave, but Hades
or the Underworld was at best a shadowy, unsatisfying place.
It had no joys to offer which could compare with the rich,
vivid life of this world. The tragedies of Greek poets are full of
pathetic speeches in which the dying say a sad farewell to the
warm, friendly light of the sun. Funeral customs demanded
the cremation of the corpse. Its ashes were then placed in a vase
or urn and buried in a cemetery which, for obvious reasons, was
always placed outside the city-walls. Here sorrowing relatives
would make offerings of mimic banquets for the refreshment

---

[1] It is true that in certain cults the worshipper adopted a different attitude;
but this was merely a relic of an old belief dating from far-away times and
connected, like human sacrifice, with the horrible demons of the Underworld
of which we spoke above (see p. 29). Such superstitions lingered on, but
they were not truly characteristic of the Greek theological outlook.

Fig. 42. MYSTIC INITIATION

This bas-relief represents the goddess Demeter, presenting the sacred
corn-ears to Triptolemus, a mythical youth, while her daughter Korê
stands by with a sacred wand.

of the departed spirit; so dependent was it still thought to be upon the material things of this more substantial world. On the gravestones which they erected were often sculptured figures, and these tell the same tale. The one pleasure of the dead is to remember the joys of earth. The man is represented as arming for battle or the chase; the woman sits with her jewellery-box. The child plays with his toys. No wonder that Greek philosophers were often sceptics or that the poets sometimes plumbed the depth of pessimism.

'*I was not, I came to be; I was, I am not; that is all; and who shall say more, will lie; I shall not be.*'

Or again: '*We all are watched and fed for Death as a herd of swine butchered wantonly.*'

Yet against these it is only justice to set one of the many superb epitaphs on fallen warriors, showing with what spirit the Greeks regarded an heroic death:

> *Setting on Hellas' brow unfading glory,*
> *These donn'd the mantle of Death's leaden gloom;*
> *Yet, dying, died not. Their high valour's story*
> *Doth so exalt them from the dismal tomb.*

One form of Greek worship, however, afforded a better hope of the life hereafter. Among the Greeks, as among most ancient peoples, there was a childlike and reverent wonder at the phenomenon of Natural Growth. When they saw the trees and plants putting forth new buds in spring-time, and after the dead winter season felt the pulse of a new life thrilling in the whole world around them, they not unnaturally believed that some unseen spirit was at work. This spirit they identified with various gods; and at Eleusis, some twelve miles from Athens, there sprang up a cult in which Dionysus the Vine-god, Demeter the Earth Mother, and other divine personages were the presiding deities. Now the celebrations of this cult were of a peculiar type. Only those who had been duly initiated were permitted to be present at its Mysteries or secret rites. Before being admitted, the candidate was required to purify himself; but such purification consisted for the most part of abstention from certain sorts of food and other forms of outward pollution. The sense of sin was not consciously a burden to the pagan mind; and the idea of a genuine moral purity of life, as we should understand it, played no real part in the preparation for the Eleusinian Mysteries.

When the day for the celebrations came round, the band of devotees collected outside the city-gate and proceeded along the Sacred Way which led to Eleusis. They were clad in white, and in their hands they carried pine-torches which, as the dusk came on, they lighted. Singing hymns to Dionysus they moved across the plain and over the intervening hills until they reached Eleusis. A day or two were spent in further ceremonial; and then, finally, in a darkened hall they were admitted to the crowning rite. There they witnessed mysterious visions which were displayed to them in flashes of light. What those visions were we cannot really tell; for the strictest secrecy was enjoined and the secret was well kept. There would appear to have been some sort of tableaux representing mythological scenes in which the deities of the cult figured. There was an exhibition of the Sacred Wheat-ear, which was clearly a symbol of the rebirth of life. What seems certain is that the devotees were not merely uplifted by some strange mood of ecstatic bliss, but that they actually obtained therefrom some assurance that all would be well with them and that, as the ear of wheat 'is not quickened except it die', so likewise through death the human soul would attain to a fuller life beyond.

Fig. 43. EDUCATION

One boy receives a lesson in writing; another in writing; a 'pedagogue' sits near by. On the wall hang (from left to right) a writing-roll, a folded tablet, a lyre, and a ruling square.

XI

EDUCATION

AT Athens the state required that all boys should be taught to read and write; girls were not catered for. It was left to parents to choose a school and to pay the fees for the class. The schools themselves were run by private enterprise; and the school-masters, as we have said, were but little respected. They often found it difficult to extract their fees. Nevertheless, the fees were low enough to allow even poor parents to get their sons tolerable instruction. Most, indeed, were not satisfied with letters alone. Music and 'gymnastics' were considered an essential part of a liberal education; and these subjects were taught in separate schools other than the grammar-schools.

To see that boys attended their classes regularly and did not get into mischief in the streets, the wealthier parents put them under the care of a slave-tutor called a 'pedagogue', and it was his duty to conduct them from class to class and to sit at the back of the room till it was time to take them home for lunch. The boys' manners and morals were his special charge. Good deportment was much esteemed. A lad was expected to rise when an older man entered the room, and to learn to hold himself correctly. It was bad manners to giggle, to grab at table, or to sit with the legs crossed.

Schooling began when a boy was six, and its elementary stage lasted until he was fourteen. In the grammar[1]-school he would learn to write with a metal instrument on a tablet of soft wax. Lessons in dictation followed. Reading was made easy by methods similar to the modern beginner's manual. Long passages from the national literature were learnt by heart. Homer was the favourite author; for his works, as we have

[1] Our word 'grammar' is derived from the Greek *gramma* (= 'a letter of the alphabet'); cp. *graphō* (= 'I write').

said, were a national institution; but the great dramatists and other poets were also studied. Explanation of difficult passages was given; and much attention was paid to recitation. In reciting, gesture would be freely used; for poetry in those days was not merely meant to be recited aloud, but acted. . . . At the grammar-master's it is probable that simple arithmetic was also taught. The Greek numerical system was extremely cumbersome, since letters of the alphabet were used in place of a decimal notation. A reckoning-board fitted with pebbles (not unlike the bead-boards which are to be seen in modern nurseries) provided valuable assistance to the beginner. . . . In the music school the flute was sometimes taught; but its wilder melodies were considered, on the whole, to be unsuitable for the young. The lyre was more popular. It was a sort of harp with seven strings which required a light touch for effective performance. Sometimes the thumb was used, sometimes a quill. Singing went with the lyre—the very term 'lyric' implies a song written for a lyre-accompaniment. There were many fine national songs; and, as we have said, an after-dinner performance was normally expected of a guest. Painting and drawing sometimes formed a part of a 'gentleman's' education, but, like music, these subjects were mainly confined to the sons of the rich.

Meanwhile, side by side with his ordinary schooling, a boy was in constant attendance at the wrestling-school or 'palaestra' kept by some professional trainer. As we have seen above, physical exercise was held to have an important influence on the development of character as well as of body. Drill and dancing were carried on to the tune of the pipe. All the different types of sport were practised, including the pancration. The *paidotribês* or teacher acted umpire in such contests, holding

WRESTLING SCENE (*see opposite*)
Two wrestlers engaged in the Pancration, one using his fist while the other attempts a throw. The trainer with stick looks on.

Fig. 44. WRESTLING SCENE

a forked stick which he would use with effect if rules were broken. The pupil's physical development was entirely in his hands. Massage was often employed as a good tonic for the muscles. A scrape and a swill-down completed the programme of a normal day. Occasionally there would be competitions in skill for which prizes were offered either by the state itself or by local associations of clansmen. Nor were the prizes confined entirely to athletics. We find rewards assigned for reading, reciting, painting, lyre-playing, and even general knowledge. There was thus plenty of incentive for boys to excel; and we have no evidence that they found their studies distasteful.

At fourteen or thereabouts poor parents would require their children's assistance in their craft or trade. The sons of the rich, however, having attained proficiency in elementary subjects, were ready to go farther; and, until they were of an age to undergo their military service, they had four years ahead of them in which to do so. Now the development of Democracy at Athens had one very significant effect. It created a thirst for knowledge; nor is it difficult to see the cause. The manifold opportunities of action and discussion sharpened men's wits. As a citizen of a self-governing community, every individual felt himself endowed with a new importance and was eager to make his way in a society which opened so many avenues to advancement. So there was a demand for fuller education; and simultaneously with the demand there had arisen a class of men competent to satisfy it. From various parts of the Greek world, and more especially from Sicily, came professional teachers who studied knowledge in all its branches. 'Sophists' or 'wisdom-mongers'[1] was the name they went by; and their claims were certainly not modest. One was prepared, for twenty pounds, to give a complete course on 'the whole duties of man'. Another was an authority on astronomy, geometry, arithmetic, grammar, and literature. He was ready to answer any question that was

[1] Hence our word 'sophistry' (= 'a clever but unfair quibble').

FIG. 45. ATHENIAN BOY

put to him; and he had invented a system whereby, if he had once heard a string of fifty names repeated, he could remember them all. Mathematics, especially geometry, was a favourite subject among sophists; and many proofs and problems, which were subsequently incorporated in Euclid's famous treatise, were already in vogue. Geography and history were also studied. But by far the most popular was instruction in Rhetoric. It was a time, as we have said, when men were anxious to make their way in the world; and, since politics and the law-courts seemed to afford the easiest way of attaining prominence, it was obvious that a training in oratory was the best passport to success. Sophists taught men how to adorn their speeches with elegant phraseology, how to work on the feelings of a jury or a mob, and above all how to argue a point. They were not very particular about the truth or falsehood of the arguments they used, and often resorted to mere quibbling. Here is a sample of sophistic logic. '*Your father is a dog,*' says one. '*So is yours,*' says another. '*Answer my questions and I'll prove it,*' says the first. '*Come now, have you a dog?*' '*Yes, and a sorry one, too.*' '*He has puppies, I take it?*' '*He has.*' '*Then the dog is a father.*' '*So it certainly seems.*' '*Well, and he is yours, is he not?*' '*Yes.*' '*So then he is a father and yours; so the dog is your father, and you are own brother to his puppies.*'

Sophists' reasoning was not, of course, always quite so farcical as this; but they were quite ready, as Aristophanes complains, to 'make the worse appear the better cause'. They gave regular courses in rhetoric, at prices varying according to the length of the course. One guaranteed in advance that, when the course was complete, the pupil would be able to win any law-suit. He was nicely caught out by a certain pupil who refused to pay up at the end, saying, '*Go to law with me if you like; but if I win, you will not get your fee, and if I lose, your guarantee will be broken and I shall not have to pay either.*'

Sometimes the sophists lectured in class-rooms; and in the

fourth century B.C. regular schools were established at the two
great gymnasia outside the walls of Athens, one under the
philosopher Plato and the other under Aristotle, his pupil. But
in the fifth century teachers were in the habit of travelling about
from city to city, and they made shift to teach their pupils in the
wrestling-schools or wherever else they could find them. The
enthusiasm they aroused, especially amongst the young, was
extraordinary. It seems that half the idle youths of Athens were
at one time occupied in drawing geometrical figures in the sand.
The characters in one of Plato's dialogues get up before dawn in
order to visit a savant who has lately arrived in the town. Often
pupils were so unwilling to abandon their studies that they would
follow their teachers to another city. Adults were scarcely less
keen. We are told that the great Pericles himself spent half a
day debating with a certain professor about an accident which
took place at some races. A horse had been killed by a chance
throw of a spear, and the question was whether the spear itself
was responsible, or the man who threw it, or the stewards who
looked after the games. Reading of books seems to have become
popular. In one play it is implied that the audience were able to
refer to a book of the words; and Plato says that a copy of a
certain philosopher's works could be bought for a very low price.
Such books were copied (as a rule by slaves) on parchment or on
papyrus brought from Egypt. The whole Athenian people seem
to have developed an inquisitive habit of mind which Aristophanes parodies in a ridiculous passage, telling how every one
was asking 'how' and 'why' and searching out the 'reasons and
the roots of things'.

> *Ay, truly, never now a man*
> *Comes home but he begins to scan,*
> *And to his household loudly cries,*
> *'Why, where's my pitcher? What's the matter?*
> *'Tis dead and gone, my dear old platter.*

K

Who gnawed these olives? Bless the sprat,
Who nibbled off the head of that?
And where's the garlic vanished, pray,
I purchased only yesterday?'

The effect of the sophists' teaching had certainly its bad side. It gave men a taste for superficial knowledge and encouraged an appeal to bare self-interest. Politicians who came under its influence argued freely that might was right; and methods of shameless aggrandizement were justified on the plea of national necessity. Needless to say, there was much debate about problems of personal conduct and morality. How is a man to find happiness? By following his instincts, said some. By living a good life, said others. What is a good life? Is it to obey the rules of society? or is it to follow what an individual's own judgement tells him to be right? One can see where such arguments would surely lead.

Among all who debated these questions the most indefatigable controversialist was the philosopher Socrates. No picture of Athenian life would be complete without some mention of this extraordinary figure—pot bellied, bald headed, snub nosed, with bulging earnest eyes which he rolled from side to side as he walked. In response to a friend's inquiry the Delphic Oracle had pronounced (even before he undertook his lifelong mission of philosophic inquiry) that Socrates was the wisest man in Greece. Greatly puzzled by this compliment, the honest fellow devoted himself to the search for a man who knew more than himself. He went about cross-examining any one who would submit to it, and discovered to his surprise that not one could give him a satisfactory answer to his searching questions. Unlike the professional sophists, he charged no fee of those who listened to his discussions; and as a result he fell into the direst poverty. Nevertheless, he did not abandon his quest. He continued to buttonhole men in the street and to discuss the problems of

FIG. 46. SOCRATES

existence with many young folk who were brought under the spell of his intellectual enthusiasm.

His normal method was always to proceed by question and answer, first persuading his interlocutor to advance some definition or opinion, then proving its absurdity by the unremitting pressure of his ruthless logic. *'What is courage?'* he would ask. *'Courage'*, the other would say, *'is the quality of a man who does not run away, but remains at his post.'* *'What, then, would you say,'* continues Socrates, *'of a man who fights flying, after the Scythian manner?'* *'That may be true of the Scythians; but the Greek hoplite, as I have said, fights remaining in his rank.'* Socrates, however, advances the instance of the Spartans at Plataea who drew the Persians out by a pretended flight; and the other is forced to propose a new definition, that courage is endurance with full knowledge of the risks. He is soon compelled to admit that a man who goes into battle well knowing his side will win is not so courageous as the man who does not know. Then, when asked if a man who descends into a well without knowing how to dive is at that rate more courageous than a man who knows, he gets completely bewildered; and so the argument runs on.

Socrates called everything in question, casting doubt on mythological stories of the behaviour of the gods and probing the motives of human conduct to their very foundations. But, destructive critic as he was of many accepted beliefs and conventions, he himself remained a faithful and devoted servant of the state, fighting stoutly on more than one battle-field. His condemnation for atheism seems to have been a gross miscarriage of justice. The charge was mainly based on the fact that he cast doubt on a multiplicity of gods and goddesses. The truth was that, like many thinkers of his own and the succeeding age, he was feeling his way towards a purer and higher conception of the deity. His pupil, Plato, from whom comes most of what we know about Socrates' views, had a more

profound theological outlook than any of the ancients except
the Hebrew prophets.

At the same time there can be little question that the teaching
of Socrates no less than the teaching of the sophists was most
unsettling, particularly to the young. Some of them, like the
notorious Alcibiades, became a real danger to the state. For,
having learnt from Socrates to call established ideas in question,
they proceeded, unlike him, to put their own theories into
practice. They followed their individual judgement as against
the traditions of the past and gave rein to their selfish instincts
at the expense of the common weal. Aristophanes complained
bitterly that the manners and morals of the younger generation
were going to the dogs. As for Alcibiades, he relapsed into an
orgy of self-indulgence and eventually turned traitor to his
country.

Thus, indirectly at any rate, the New Learning of the sophists
was to prove the ruin of Greece. Slowly but surely it sapped
the strength of her people's character. In the succeeding epoch
the old sense of allegiance to the state decayed. Men no longer
placed the common welfare before their personal interest. Even
the Athenians grew lazy and preferred to hire mercenary troops
to fight their wars for them. The private houses of the rich began
to vie in splendour with public monuments. The history of the
fourth century is one sordid tale of mean intrigues, spiteful
revenges, and unscrupulous diplomacy. Each man tended to
become a law to himself; and the bonds which held the city-
state together were gradually loosened.

Such was the mournful outcome of the New Enlightenment.
Yet it had its nobler and more enduring side. For Socrates'
example was not wholly lost upon his countrymen. His pupil
Plato and other great philosophers carried on his earnest and
sincere pursuit of truth; and thus, while the political life of
Greece was ruined, her intellectual life received a stimulus and
inspiration which was to influence the thinkers of all succeeding

time. For Socrates had taught them to trust their reason. *'We must follow whither the argument will lead'* was one of his favourite maxims; and wherever men have learnt to think honestly and to think straight, they have been in a very real sense his pupils.

NOTE.—Most of our English vocabulary which has to do with education is derived from the Greek. Thus, 'philosophy' is from *philo* (I love) and *sophia* (wisdom); 'logic' is the science of *logoi* or words; 'mathematics' originally meant the science of things learnt or discovered; 'geometry' is the measuring of *gê* = the earth; 'geography' the drawing (*grapho* = draw or write) of the earth; 'arithmetic' is the science of *arithmoi* or numbers. 'Physics' is derived from *physis* = nature; and nearly the whole vocabulary of the scientific laboratory will be found to be derived from the Greeks, the first scientists.

CONCLUSION

IT was Pericles' ideal that Athens should be 'an education to Greece'; and there can be no doubt that his ideal was fulfilled in actual fact. Indeed, we can scarcely question that in intelligence, in taste, and in enthusiastic zeal to be up and doing the Athenians as a body have found no equals in the history of the world. A modern psychologist has declared that 'the average intelligence of the Athenian race was as much higher than our own as our own is higher than that of the African negro'. Consider the range of the average Athenian's activities. On their public side, he was a practical politician, an administrator of the law, very possibly a speaker, and quite certainly a soldier or a sailor. If not himself an artist or a craftsman, he was at least capable of appreciating the beauty of others' work; and all that he did he performed with a zest and enterprise which kept him young and vigorous. He practised athletics all his days. He could sing, dance, and play the lyre. He had a thirst for

THE GODDESS ATHENA

She is represented leaning on her spear and looking at a
gravestone. She may be reading the names of the citizens
who had recently fallen in defence of her city.

knowledge and discussed incessantly the deeper problems of human existence.

Let us hear what Pericles himself had to say about his country-men. *'Ours'*, he said, as Thucydides records of him, *'ours is no workaday city. No other provides so many recreations of the spirit—contests and sacrifices all the year round, and beauty in our public buildings to cheer the spirit and delight the eye. We are lovers of beauty without extravagence, lovers of wisdom without loss of manliness. Our citizens attend both to public and private duties, allowing no absorption in their own affairs to interfere with their knowledge of the city's. The man who holds aloof from public life, we regard as useless. We are noted for being at once the most adventurous in action and the most reflective in preparation therefor. We yield to none, man by man, for independence of spirit, many-sidedness of attainment, and complete self-reliance in limbs and brain. Great, indeed, are the symbols of our supremacy. For our pioneers have forced their way into every corner of sea or land, establishing among mankind eternal memorials of their settle-ment.'*

The speech from which these extracts have been quoted was delivered by Pericles in memory of the Athenians who had fallen during the first year of the Peloponnesian War against Sparta. He himself died shortly afterwards; but the war ran on. At the end of ten years a peace was patched up, but it proved short-lived; and soon Athens, overreaching herself in her ambition, embarked on the tremendous adventure of invading Sicily. The disaster which there befell her fleet was the beginning of her decline. Taking advantage of the catastrophe, many of her subject-allies revolted. Persia, still a jealous and watchful enemy, assisted them and Sparta by financing the construction of an efficient fleet; and eventually, in a great naval battle fought at Aegospotami in 405 B.C., Athens lost her command of the sea. By the stern conditions which were subsequently imposed upon her she was utterly humbled. Her ships were taken from her;

even her Long Walls were razed. Her chance of uniting all Greece under her leadership was gone for ever.

Throughout the first half of the following century the history of the country was nothing better than an interminable dog-fight between state and state. At first Sparta was 'top dog'; then Thebes. At one time even Athens resumed some pretensions to a maritime supremacy. But a more powerful than any of these was presently to emerge. Far away on the northern frontier of the Greek peninsula lay the half-civilized people of Macedon. Their king, Philip, was a man of vast ambition and iron character. Out of his wild fellow tribesmen he created a first-rate army. By tireless pertinacity he strove to ingratiate himself with the Greeks, who at first despised him as an outsider. At last he found the opportunity to intervene in their midst, being summoned by one party to decide a religious quarrel. Athens and Thebes, realizing the peril, determined to oppose him; but at Chaeronea in 338 B.C. their armies suffered overwhelming defeat. This was the end of Greek freedom. The country lay under the heel of Macedon.

It can scarcely be denied that the Greeks had deserved their fate. The interminable feuds between state and state had utterly exhausted their strength. Within the states themselves, the sense of patriotism and unity had been sapped by tendencies of which we spoke above. This quick-witted folk had developed their intelligence at the expense of their character. They had disputed, intrigued, and overreached one another till the life of the city-state had been poisoned at the root. One is tempted to say that their vaunted intellectualism had proved a miserable fiasco; and so in a sense it might have been if this had been the end. But it was not the end. On the death of Philip, his son Alexander, having succeeded to the throne, set out to conquer the East. He swiftly overran the Persian Empire, and round the coasts of the Levant he established new centres of Greek civilization. In these centres, and especially at Alexandria in

Egypt, the culture of Greece received a new lease of life. The work of philosophers and scientists was carried on with a fresh vigour. Many practical discoveries, in medicine and other arts, were the result; and the prestige of these new seats of learning threw even decadent Athens into the shade. Now, in course of time, Rome began to extend her conquests eastwards. Till then her people, though warlike, had been almost completely boorish and illiterate. But as, step by step, they came in contact with peoples of Greek culture they too fell under its spell. Greek teachers poured into Italy. Greek art, literature, and thought were studied; and from Greek models all that the Romans themselves were able to achieve in these fields was directly or indirectly derived. Finally, as her Empire spread, and her civilization with it, Rome handed on to the peoples of western Europe the heritage which she had herself received from Greece. Thus, while it may be true that the Greeks destroyed their own country in the process of thinking things out, they had none the less set something in motion which was of infinite consequence to all posterity. For, had it not been for their thinking, it can hardly be doubted that we ourselves should still be living in a condition of gross superstition and semi-barbarism. There is no evidence that Gauls, Spaniards, or Britons would have been capable of making the forward step for themselves.

It is to the Greeks, then, that we owe to-day by far the greater part of our intellectual and artistic heritage. Especially since the Renaissance of the sixteenth century, when scholars and thinkers were greatly influenced by the rediscovery of Greek literature, almost wholly neglected during the Middle Ages, the debt has been redoubled. How great that debt is it would be difficult to exaggerate. Half the buildings in London, or any great town, are designed in styles invented by Greek architects. Since the Renaissance the greatest masters of sculpture have been inspired by the work of Greek artists. From Greek authors the arts of history and biography have been derived. Oratory,

as we know it, came originally from Greece. Drama, especially
the French drama, has been much influenced by the Attic
tragedians. There is scarcely one of the great poets who was
not in some sense a debtor to the Greeks. But, above all, the
thought of the Western World takes its spring and origin from
them. The creed of the Christian Church was formulated in
terms drawn from the Greek philosophers. Modern science
took its starting-point in the study of long-forgotten Greek
treatises. The ideas of Plato and Aristotle lie at the back of all
modern attempts to solve the problems of Life and the Universe.
In a word, the Greek spirit has been the stimulus and inspiration
of all honest inquiry after truth.

What the Greek spirit was we have endeavoured to convey in
the preceding pages. Its essence was an ardent belief in the
free exercise of the human faculties—freedom, that is, for every
man to take his share in the direction of his country's destiny;
freedom to enjoy the activities of mind and body with which
Nature has provided him; freedom, above all, to follow the
dictates of his own reasoning powers. And just because the
Greek was willing to trust his reason and 'follow whither the
argument might lead', he was able to see, more clearly than most
men have seen, what is really worth while in life. True, he had
his limitations, and very serious limitations they were. There
were many elements of coarseness and cruelty in his character.
He was blind to the inhumanity of slavery and the degradation
of his womenfolk. The specifically Christian virtues formed no
part of his moral make-up. But, apart from these limitations,
he 'saw life steadily and saw it whole'. He knew what made
for a full and happy life—healthy exercise of body, skill of hand
and energy of brain, the zest of a congenial occupation and the
enjoyment of a leisure well used for the appreciation of the beautiful, the society of friends, and a vigorous interchange of ideas.
It is difficult to feel that the average Englishman of the twentieth
century has an equally clear conception of life's opportunities.

GLOSSARY OF GREEK NAMES, ETC.

(N.B. Pronounce ch *hard* as in ache)

Achĭl'lēs
Acrŏp'ŏlis
Aegis'thus
Aegŏspŏt'ămi
Ae'schylus
Ăgămem'non
Ăg'ăthon
Ăg'ŏra
Alcĭbī'ădēs
Alcĭn'ŏus
Alphĕsĭboe'a
Andrŏm'ăchē
Ăpătur'ia
Arēs
Arĕŏp'ăgus
Aristŏdē'mus
Aristŏph'ănēs
Asclē'pius
Athē'nă or Athē'nē

Chaerŏnē'a
Chā'ron
Clytemnēs'tra

Dēlos
Dēmē'ter
Demŏcē'dēs

Dēmŏs'thĕnēs
Dĭŏnȳ'sus

Ēleu'sis
Ephē'boi
Eurĭp'ĭdēs
Eurō'tas

Hā'dēs
Hēphae'stus
Hĕrŏdŏ'tus
Hippŏc'rătēs
Hȳmet'tus

Ĭlĭad
Iphĭgĕnei'a

Lăcĕdae'mon
Lau'rĕum
Lĕŏn'ĭdas
Lȳcur'gus
Lȳs'ĭas

Mĕg'ărŏn
Mĕtic
Mī'notaur
Mȳcē'nae

Nausĭc'äa
Nĭ'cĭas

Ŏd'ȳssey

Pănăthĕnae'a
Păncrăt'ĭon
Par'thĕnon
Pĕl'ŏpŏnnēse
Pĕnĕl'ŏpē
Pentĕl'ĭcus
Pĕr'ĭclēs
Phei'dias
Pŏlȳclī'tus
Pŏsei'don
Praxĭt'ĕlēs

Săl'ămis
Soc'rătēs
Sŏph'ŏclēs
Sphactē'ria
Strĕpsĭ'ădēs

Taȳ'gĕtus
Thermop'ȳlae
Thūcȳd'ĭdēs

Xanthip'pē
Xĕn'ŏphon
Xer'xēs

INDEX

Achaeans, 11.
Acharnae, 90.
Achilles, 14, 16, 23, 28; verses on his shield, 17, 18, 20.
Acropolis, 50, 56, 102, 104, 108, 111, 120.
actors, 122, 124, 126, 128.
Aegospotami, 151.
Aeschylus, 128.
Agamemnon, 29.
Agathon, 80.
Agora, the, 73.
agriculture, 16, 89.
Alcibiades, 149.
Alcinous, 16, 25, 28.
Alexander the Great, 74, 153.
Alphesiboea, 18.
anatomy, 99, 108.
Andromache, 28.
'Answerer', 122.
Apaturia, 133.
Apollo, 29, 30.
architecture, 102.
archon, 55.
Areopagus, 57.
Ares, 30.
Argive Plain, 12.
Aristodemus, 80.
Aristophanes, 67, 80, 88, 91, 98, 111, 129, 144, 149.
Aristotle, 87, 145, 155.
arithmetic, 140, 150.
armour, 22, 43.
Asclepius, 99.
astrologers, 98.
Athena, 29, 30, 108.
Athens, 29, 47 ff.
athletics, 28, 38, 111–18, 140, 142.
athlon, 111.

Bacchus, 81, 130.
ball games, 111.
banquets, 78.
'barbarians', 95.

barber's shop, 74.
baths, 71, 76.
battering-rams, 44.
betrothals, 82.
books, 145.
boxing, 114.
branding, 87.
'Bronze Fly', 111.
building, 102.

carts, 98.
cattle, 18.
cavalry, 44.
Cerameicus, 100.
Chaeronea, 153.
charcoal-burners, 90.
chariot races, 116.
chariots, 98.
charms, 130.
Charon, 94.
chorus, the, 124.
Citadel, 68.
city-state, 31.
Cleon, 53, 54, 55.
climate, 68, 71.
clothes, 44, 68, 74.
cock-fighting, 111.
coins, 92–4.
comedy, 126, 129.
conversation, 72.
Corinth, 92, 98.
Corinthian architecture, 104.
corn, 90.
'Cottabos', 80.
craftsmen, 16, 81.
cremation, 134.
Crete, 11, 29.
crime, 57.
Crypteia, 40.

dancing, 26, 78, 112, 140.
Dardanelles, 14.
darics, 92.
death, 134.
Delian League, 50.
Delos, 50.
Delphi, 29, 30, 119.

Delphic oracle, 132.
demagogues, 53.
'deme', 55, 59.
Demeter, 135.
Democedes, 99.
democracy, 51.
dice, 111.
Dionysia, the Great, 120.
Dionysus, 120, 135–6.
doctors, 99.
Dorians, 30, 35.
Doric architecture, 103, 104.
dowry, 84.
drachma, 93.
drainage, 71, 110.
dramatic entertainments, 120–9.
draughts, 111, 113.
drawing, 140.
dreams, 130.
drilling, 112, 140.
drinking, 77–81.
drinking-songs, 80.

Ecclesia, 52.
education, 36, 138–50.
Egypt, 20, 22.
Egyptians, 32.
Eleusinian Mysteries, 137.
Epheboi, 60.
Ephors, 35.
Epidaurus, 125.
Euripides, 128, 129.
Eurotas, river, 35, 38.
eyes, treatment of, 74.

farmers, 81.
festal celebrations, 120.
fighting, *see* warfare.
flogging, 36, 87.
food, 42, 70, 74, 76–81.
funeral customs, 134.
furniture, 71.

games, 80, 111–18.
geography, 144.